TRUE NORTH

Finding Your Life's Purpose

PAUL FENTON-SMITH

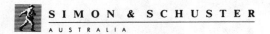

SIMON & SCHUSTER

AUSTRALIA

TRUE NORTH: FINDING YOUR LIFE'S PURPOSE
First published in Australia in 2002
Simon & Schuster (Australia) Pty Limited
20 Barcoo Street, East Roseville NSW 2069

A Viacom Company
Sydney New York London

Visit our website at www.simonsaysaustralia.com

National Library of Australia
Cataloguing-in-Publication data

Fenton-Smith, Paul
    True north. Finding your life's purpose

    ISBN 0 7318 1147 X.

    1. Self-actualization (Psychology). 2. Conduct of Life. 3. Quality of Life
    I. Title.

    158.1

Cover and internal design: Avril Makula GRAVITY AAD
Typeset in Caslon 11 pt on 14 pt
Printed in Australia by Griffin Press

10 9 8 7 6 5 4 3 2 1

TRUE NORTH

Dedicated to Alexander, whose company improves the journey immensely.

With thanks to Cathy for her editing skills, and to Korina for her patience.

Contents

Preface

Do you seek a more meaningful path in life? Your true path in life is likely to be more than a suitable career or a compatible love relationship. It is a path that furthers your spiritual growth and one that leaves you feeling more passionate about life.

Using sailing as a metaphor for life, this book examines why many people sail off course or stray from their life's purpose. While others may assist you in your search for purpose, it is a search that only you can complete. In navigating your own course in life, you gain strengths and experience that are necessary for the successful conclusion to your life's quest.

Even when you have found your purpose and are happily sailing towards it, the wind sometimes drops. In these cases you either wait for another breeze or adjust your sails to make the most of a breeze from a different direction. This occurred with Sally, who had enjoyed a successful career in television for 20 years. Having worked in several areas within the industry, she found herself without employment for eight months. She began to question if she'd ever work in the industry again. With help, Sally searched for new openings and adjusted her direction according to life's opportunities; resuming her chosen career. It was as though she had unfurled a different sail and caught a breeze from a new direction.

It's not all smooth sailing. You are likely to encounter storms, cloudy days and wild seas between the sunny periods. On your journey through life you may encounter pirates, discover tropical islands and other sailing vessels, varying from flimsy rafts to ocean liners crammed with people sharing a journey. You may visit crowded, chaotic and even abandoned ports.

If true north is true purpose in life, how do you find it? The whole journey hinges on this one simple question. Where is true north for you?

People around you, locations, situations and even institutions cannot be a reliable guide for true north for you. You can only find true purpose within. Parents, teachers and university lecturers often speak with authority, and it can be tempting to see life through their eyes and according to their compasses. They may guide you, yet they cannot take your journey for you.

True north is essentially true purpose. With clarity of purpose, former distractions become mere background chatter to your life's work. People who may have once distracted you from your purpose become witnesses to your map-making skills.

Having someone close who truly believes in you can be a great advantage in the pursuit of your goals and your purpose. From a parent or teacher to a supportive partner or a friend, most successful and contented people have had some support and encouragement along the way. The Beatles had Brian Epstein and George Martin, and many great painters and musicians throughout history had patrons or mentors to encourage and to guide them towards success.

If you don't currently have someone who truly believes in you, then perhaps it's time to find a support group for the skills you want to develop or the path you seek to take. Engaging an experienced private tutor, a counsellor or a life coach can benefit you in the pursuit of your life's purpose. This can allow you to share your burdens or to bounce new ideas around with someone who has your best interests at heart.

A well-lived life is like a well-drawn map. Whether it charts a grand public life on the open seas or a small, untroubled existence in an unknown bay, such a life serves to show one clear path for others who may be lost and searching for a port.

A purposeful life is worth every step you take in overcoming obstacles, climbing mountains and descending into the valleys of life. Life filled with purpose is like a sleek yacht, seeking the assistance of the wind on its journey, as it glides across a glistening sea.

CHAPTER ONE

A Viable Starting Point

Do you have a pressing urgency of the journey ahead to fulfil your life's purpose wothout a starting point or the sense of the direction of that journey? You don't have to discover your purpose because a part of you already knows it. You only have to become acquainted with the part of you which knows your true purpose and heed its directions. This part of you gladly imparts its knowledge to you, if you are prepared to spend the time to listen. To listen, you need to be very still, both physically and mentally. The metaphor below is to show you how your purpose may be illuminated if you are still enough to hear that part of you.

Imagine that you have purchased a large old home, set in two hectares of gardens on the edge of a city. It comprises a large cellar, six bedrooms, enormous entertainment areas, a lawn tennis court, a swimming pool and a traditional summerhouse covered in wisteria and set in a rose garden. The two-car garage adjoins the house. One afternoon while you're in the garage you notice a rusty old lever protruding from a wall. Your curiosity is aroused and you attempt to push the lever down to see what will result from this. It is rusted hard. You spray some oil onto the lever, returning the following day. On a second attempt, the lever slides downwards, and a previously hidden door opens in the wall of the garage. Behind the door is a staircase leading up to a large room that is part-den and part-laboratory, still filled with the possessions of the previous owner, now deceased. This room is set back from the outer walls of the house, so it was not visible from the grounds. When you purchased the house, the room was not listed in the plans, which means that no-one was aware of its existence except perhaps the builder. Small windows are set high in the walls to offer light, but not a view over the gardens. This is a room offering a place to ponder and to invent. Although it affords you no immediate view over the property, it does offer you a perfect view of your life. While in this room, you remain undistracted, hidden from everyone else in the house or in the grounds.

Each of us already has such a room within us. All we need do is locate the secret door to access it. The location of the door varies according to the person, and the fact that you have not found it does not invalidate the existence of the 'hidden room'. The room's contents vary according to each of us. When I first discovered the room in a dream one night, it occurred to me that inspiration for an almost unlimited number of books was to be found while sitting there. In my dream, I experienced a profound sense of clarity. My life's purpose was as clear to me as the objects in the room, including an old record player I was examining on a table. I felt stillness descend. Although I had a deep sense of my life's purpose, I felt no urgent need to pursue it at that moment. I was too busy noticing the feeling of completeness that comes from knowing what I had to do and how I was to do it. Excitement, anticipation and contentment engulfed me in turn.

Each of us deserves to experience stillness and clarity of purpose regularly, for the motivation needed to replenish our flagging spirits when we feel beaten down by life as we attempt to make our purpose real. Knowing your purpose doesn't guarantee that you'll fulfil it. It simply gives you something meaningful to work towards.

Your purpose doesn't have to be exceedingly original. Nor does it need to be acceptable to those whose opinions you value. You don't need to share it with those around you. Your purpose is your own.

I have a friend, Jean-Pierre, whose purpose is to fade to grey, in order not to be distracted by others from his meditation. He doesn't work, socialise, drink alcohol or encourage community interaction. Instead, he grows his own herbs, vegetables and fruit, trading some of these for grains and other basic supplies. He lives an almost monastic life, yet he is filled with a sense of purpose.

He is an example of how having this purpose makes it easier to forsake those things we reward ourselves with when we are without purpose. He finds it easy not to smoke, drink, socialise or work in a day-to-day job, because he does not need these things to lend him a sense of purpose. He doesn't need them to distract him from a lack of purpose. Very few people share his views about solitary life, but it works very well for him. He is content. While those he meets are often carrying unfulfilled desires, Jean-Pierre is inwardly still. He radiates a quiet contentment.

When many of us think of a sense of purpose, we think of saving the world, healing the sick — making an enormous difference to humanity in some way. Does purpose have to be huge? It may be your purpose to save the world, heal the sick or otherwise make an enormous difference to humanity, yet whether your purpose affects many or few, it is still your purpose. It's unlikely this purpose stems from your ego. It often bears no relation to your ambitions, emanating rather from some deeper place where it already resides. In quiet moments, when your mind is still, you can hear that small voice within, whispering to you. You may ask one or two significant questions relating to the fulfilment of your purpose at these times. Resist the temptation to ask for lottery numbers or about goals that only require your commitment to be realised. Instead, use such moments to clarify the next step on your path.

This doesn't mean that you won't need to make strenuous efforts to realise your dreams. Rather, the fulfilment of your purpose is so important that the physical steps are welcomed, as each step brings you closer to the realisation of that purpose.

CHAPTER TWO

Loss of Purpose

You can be distracted from your purpose by those around you, but life, too, can fling you from your path through trauma, loss, ill health or overwhelming responsibilities.

An example of this occurred with Adrian, whose father left the family home when the boy was seven. The boy never saw him again. Soon afterwards, Adrian became responsible for his younger sisters, for the house, even for paying the bills when his mother sank into depression, not venturing out for two years. His mother's sister helped out on a weekly basis, but any sense of purpose Adrian once had was obscured by his new responsibilities.

He was 44 years of age before he ceased feeling responsible for others and began to ponder his own purpose. By 46, Adrian knew what he wanted to be. All those years of hard work and responsibility had served him well, for he was disciplined enough to return to study, to undertake and to complete his law degree. It didn't happen without effort, and there were a few people who were disappointed that Adrian wasn't helping them out as he once had, but his purpose was greater than his sense of guilt at abandoning those who had grown to rely upon him.

Sometimes loss of purpose occurs in a gradual fashion. You begin with a small compromise and then another. Soon you have taken several steps away from your intended path in life, and you're wondering where the sense of fulfilment has gone. Often, however, even when you do lose your way, you are given reminders as to the way back to your path. These might come in the form of dreams, or from friends encouraging you to pursue your goals or even from ill health. Each of us is reminded in a different way.

Real purpose is accompanied by a conviction and the courage to fulfil it.

Peter sinks into depression whenever he wanders too far from his path. He loves to draw, and he has been a successful artist for many years. Occasionally, he forgets his purpose and stops drawing. Soon he becomes restless, irritable and, eventually, withdrawn. Not long after this he sinks into a state of depression, crying on and off for days.

After this period of tears and anguish, Peter takes up a pen and begins drawing. Often it is something simple at first. Perhaps, inspired by a colourful bird in a nearby tree, he takes to sketching. Before long he is immersed in a variety of mediums, including oils, watercolours and pen and ink.

Stillness descends as Peter remembers his purpose again. Despite being exhausted from his recent depression, he is enlivened by a sense of purpose, of hope and the knowledge that what he is doing is right for him. After the first day of drawing, Peter usually sleeps well, and soon he is arranging his next exhibition, confident in his ability to complete enough work to fill the gallery on the day. It is possible that, being an artist, Peter is more sensitive than most to the distractions of life, but gradually he is realising that the pursuit of purpose demands sacrifices.

It's not that we lose our sense of purpose every now and then that matters; what counts is that we eventually find it again. Also important is the effect of the decisions we make during any period of lack of purpose. For example, during that time, we may decide to invest in a new house to make life more worthwhile. When rediscovering our purpose, we still have to repay the mortgage, despite perhaps no longer desiring the house.

Expect to lose sight of your purpose occasionally. Anticipate inner hunger which stems from not feeding yourself spiritually, and be vigilant for the opportunity to take a path back to your purpose when it appears.

Sometimes we feel so lost and tired in our prolonged search for purpose, that we need the assistance of others. Often a teacher, a counsellor, a healer or simply someone with good powers of observation can assist us in relocating it. Finding the right person to assist us can be a challenge.

Yvette, a mother of three, was dealing with a rebellious eleven-year-old son after her husband had left and moved overseas. Deciding that the boy might flourish in a military school, she enrolled him. Three years later, in an update on his progress, Yvette informed me that he had been moved to a military boarding school, where he was thriving. With routines and positive role models, he was excelling in sports and had a wide circle of new friends.

Remaining observant of life's signs is also important in the pursuit of purpose. Resisting the urge to read meaning into each and every insignificant event, we can notice which occurrences are signs for us to follow. Real purpose is accompanied by a conviction and the courage to fulfil it. It is rare to glimpse your purpose easily, yet with effort we can uncover purpose for our journey on earth.

CHAPTER THREE

Short- and Long-term Purpose

In the last 100 years, it seems that Western civilisation has lost faith in religion and in government, with the result that we now have a diminished sense of purpose in the world.

Without purpose, we tend to seek out diversions from the emptiness that pervades our lives. We have created and invented a huge assortment of them, including shopping, computer games, television and fiction reading. In the end, these don't offer lasting fulfilment.

In my work as a counsellor, I am repeatedly faced with people who lack a sense of purpose — in their lives and in their careers. These capable, talented people are without any long-term sense of purpose to motivate them towards goals they can achieve.

Purpose can be divided into three categories:

- DAILY PURPOSE. This is what motivates us to get up in the morning, to meet our daily challenges enthusiastically. It can be rewarded by the sense of accomplishment that comes from reflecting on a job well done at the end of the day.

- **YEARLY PURPOSE.** Longer-term purpose enables us to make short-term sacrifices in order to achieve its goals. You might cut back your spending in order to save for an overseas holiday or a deposit on a car. You might begin weekly counselling sessions in order to resolve the past and prepare you for an improved emotional life.

- **LIFE PURPOSE.** This is the sense of what you have come into this life to do, learn or understand. It can make longer-term difficulties more bearable. An awareness of your life's purpose can give your life added meaning, leaving you less inclined to seek pointless diversions that offer only momentary fulfilment.

To better understand if you have a sense of purpose on each of these three levels, try the questionnaire below:

- Do you have a sense of where you belong in your local community?

- Despite the routine nature of daily work, do you approach your day with a positive sense of purpose?

- Do you reflect upon your daily achievements and frustrations at the close of the day?

- Do you have a sense that each year in your life is bringing you closer to your life's purpose?

Sometimes the frustration that builds when we contemplate our circumstances forces us not to think too long about life. Although this helps to reduce blood pressure on a daily basis, it doesn't help to address those circumstances.

- What is your primary purpose today?

- Are you easily distracted from your daily purpose?

- What is your primary purpose this year?

- How will you know when you've realised this purpose?

- Will you review your progress throughout the year?

- Are you easily distracted from your yearly purpose?

Reviewing progress is similar to checking the map when driving on a long journey. To ensure that you haven't taken a wrong turn, you check regularly. Doing the same with your goals and purpose helps to ensure that you arrive at your destination.

- What is your primary purpose in life?

- How did you discover this purpose?

- If you haven't discovered it, how do you plan to discover it?

- Are you easily distracted from finding or from pursuing your life's purpose?

- What sort of distraction sways you?

Knowing with a sense of certainty what you are here to do today, this year and this lifetime can mean the difference between being frustrated and fulfilled by daily life.

I've observed that most people have more energy or can persevere with problems much longer when they have a sense of purpose. It is as though they are prepared to push harder to ascend a hill, knowing that a clear view of their surroundings awaits them at the summit.

It's not that important what your purpose is, only that you have a sense of it and act on it. One example is Rosalie, who has devoted 22 years of her life to being a mother. In her heart, she knows that the efforts she has made will last generations and perhaps affect dozens of people.

Another example of purpose is Thomas, whose childhood was marred by a violent father and a rough neighbourhood. As a teenager, he learned a martial art, which led him to feeling safe and in control of his life for the first time. After seven years he felt the need to share the sense of centredness he experienced with others, so he established a martial arts school to teach others how to feel strong and in control of their lives. Today he has a thriving school. He travels internationally, studying and teaching martial arts.

Most people find they have more energy or can persevere with problems much longer when they have a sense of purpose.

Often those things that most scarred us as children become a part of our purpose or, at least, sharpen our need to find purpose. In the business section of a newspaper, I read of a man whose company was one of the leading home builders in England. He was proud of his efforts to give buyers of his homes the quality of life he felt they deserved. This man had been adopted by a family of gypsies from a Barnados home as a child. He had left school with difficulty in reading and writing. Yet, at the time of the article, his business had a market value of £1 billion. 'It's great to take a piece of land and turn it into a living and breathing thing,' he said. Perhaps his own experiences as a child led him to value the benefits of a stable home and home life. Conceivably, his childhood fashioned within him a sense of purpose. (*The Weekly Telegraph*, Issue 495, Jan 17th 2001)

Many of us are obliged to work at a job that does not further our life's purpose but simply pays the bills and allows us to survive. A vicious circle develops. To improve self-esteem, we distract ourselves from the inner voice with rewards, such as a new car, a holiday or a bigger house, and soon we are chained to the job we dislike.

It's easy to say, 'Just quit', but if you've ever just quit a job and discovered what it is like to be penniless, you know that it can be a harrowing experience. It's not easy pursuing your life's purpose when you are starving and marginalised by society because you do not have a job and a regular income.

However, we need to have a sense of life purpose before we can direct ourselves toward a yearly purpose, or have a rewarding daily purpose. To glimpse that life purpose, it is necessary to release any mental and emotional baggage from the past that may obscure or colour our view. Sometimes this means we have to work on past unresolved issues.

To successfully realise your purpose, you need to remain aware of both short- and long-term purpose. It is similar to pacing yourself for a marathon, so as not to tire too early. The following points may assist you in this endeavour:

- Review your short- and long-term goals.

- Decide if these goals are leading you towards or away from your true purpose in life.

- Adjust or remove those goals which may hinder your pursuit of life purpose.

- Review your short-term goals regularly (weekly or monthly).

- Review your long-term goals regularly, such as yearly (but not on New Year's Eve after you've consumed two bottles of a fabulous champagne).

- Adjust your efforts if and when necessary to remain on the path to your purpose.

CHAPTER FOUR

The Past

It is important to focus on the past, because that's where you have packed all the baggage that may weigh your boat down presently, as you sail towards your purpose. It is time to ask yourself some difficult questions. Some people and situations in your life may be unwanted baggage. If so, it is time to decide if you still wish to carry it around. Completing the following questionnaire may help:

- Do any of your friends constitute baggage in your life now? Have you outgrown a friendship, but still feel obliged to continue with it?

- Is your job baggage or does it meet your needs?

- Is your home baggage?

- Is your town or city baggage in your life right now?

- Be aware that before you discard any of the above, you'll need to replace them further down the track. Choose carefully, as you'll be living with the consequences of your choices and actions.

Past baggage includes habits you steadfastly cling to, expectations you have not yet surrendered and your beliefs about life.

Habits are those annoying little repetitive pastimes that make up a day and then a week and then a lifetime and yet lend a sense of security to your existence. Some habits are beneficial and need not be challenged. What needs to be examined is that collection of outdated rituals and repetitive behaviours that prevent you from sailing smoothly forward in life.

When you sit for a while scanning your life for unnecessary habits, chances are you'll miss many of them. A friend who was desperate to save money once spent a week writing down on a pad every single purchase he made that one week. He didn't judge what he was doing, nor did he question it. He simply wrote it down to be reviewed at a later date. When he did review it, he was amazed at the number of habits he hadn't realised he still had from his past. One of these was a love of soft drinks and fruit juices.

'Do you know that I spent over $35 in a week on soft drinks?' he asked me, perplexed at how this could be so.

Many habits are invisible to the person performing them, remaining below conscious awareness. We go through the motions unaware. This explains the man in the car next to you who sits picking his teeth, staring into the sunset, while stationary at traffic lights.

Keeping an accurate diary of the events of each day is one way to highlight your unconscious habits. Another way is to have someone else point out your habits to you. I'm not suggesting you ask your friends or family to do this (although I'm sure they'd jump at the chance to tell you honestly what they think ...).

Consulting a counsellor or a life coach gives you the chance to have your negative habits highlighted in a tactful and positive way. You are then encouraged and supported while you change or replace the habits with more beneficial ones.

Negative habits are like weeds in a garden. Once you control them, the effort required to keep them to a minimum is not too demanding. Weeds are any plants you don't want or have too many of in your garden. As with habits, what constitutes a weed varies from place to place.

Where I grew up, people planted cacti and bamboo cane in their gardens. Where I live presently, bamboo cane is classified as a rampant weed and is banned. Not too far from here, cacti are also classified as a weed and are prohibited. In other words, what is classed as a bad habit in some places is encouraged in others. While creativity is discouraged in accountancy (although some people may actively seek a creative accountant to reduce their tax liability) it is actively encouraged in the arts.

Since habits are learned, new habits can be learned to replace the old patterns. However, the more ingrained the habit, the longer it takes to be replaced. An example of this is Rupert, who grew up in a working-class town in England. At the first opportunity, he left for London. There he spent several years replacing his original accent with a more subtle one. In his mind, this would enable him to rise in his chosen career.

Indeed, Rupert's accent is flawless — until he drinks. After a bottle of champagne, his accent loses its edge. Deep into the second bottle, he reverts to his old speech patterns. In another ten years, it is likely that even when drinking, Rupert won't revert to his original accent, because the new one is becoming even more ingrained.

Before you can commence your journey, you need to re-examine your baggage to see if you really need to carry it all with you. Expectations are baggage, too, although these may be even less visible than habits. What we have learned to expect from ourselves and from life shapes not only our journey but the vessel we sail in.

When opportunities beckon, do you run to them and examine them carefully? Or do you turn away, telling yourself that they are not for you? Expectation isn't shaped only in your mind; it is often forged in your body. Your body alerts you when you are uncomfortable with a situation, with a level of success or with the amount of praise, attention or reward you are receiving for your efforts. When you listen to your body, it is easy to realise what your expectations of life are.

It is your body that tells you it is uncomfortable about taking an exam, or consulting a doctor or jumping out of a plane with a parachute strapped to your back. At these times your mind is often rationalising away the fears you feel within your physical body.

Some years ago, Terry was preparing scrambled eggs for breakfast as his six-year-old daughter Jesse sat at the table playing with a toy. Ten minutes later, he placed a plate of toast and scrambled eggs down in front of her. She approached it enthusiastically but, two minutes later, placed the fork onto the plate and burst into tears.

'What's wrong?' Terry asked her.

'This isn't scrambled eggs.'

'Yes it is.'

'But it's not how Mummy makes it.'

Terry knew that he had to rescue the situation, as he had no idea what Jesse's mother did for her version of scrambled eggs, so he decided to change the girl's expectations.

'Well of course it isn't. Mummy is from England and she makes English scrambled eggs. I make them the French way.'

'The French way?' Jesse asked, wiping her eyes.

'Yes. Dominic taught me in a tiny hostel high in the Pyrenees mountains.' At this point Terry launched into a story about backpacking through France and living on baguettes, grilled fish and French wines. Jesse resumed eating her eggs as he spoke.

Now in Jesse's mind, Terry's eggs weren't better or worse than her mother's, but different. (Of course, there will be more tears when she visits France and discovers that no-one cooks eggs the way Dominic did.)

Beliefs about yourself and about life are invisible when you search for them, but completely apparent when you seek them out through their manifestations. In other words, although beliefs conceal themselves from our gaze, we can decipher them by observing the life we lead. In fact, they often shape our lives by influencing our perception of opportunities, threats, challenges and responsibilities. So by observing how we deal with these four groupings, we can better understand our core beliefs.

An example of how core beliefs can limit perception of opportunities is provided by a client named William, who came for hypnosis to help him to become a famous ballet dancer. He was specific about his goal. We sat together to identify what he had previously done to reach it. He outlined the years spent learning, practising and performing. He described his frustration at not landing the bigger roles he felt he deserved.

What we have learned to expect from ourselves and from life shapes not only our journey but the vessel we sail in.

William had put considerable effort into dance training. He'd also embraced the dancer's lifestyle, which, in itself, is often too much for many aspiring dancers. He was physically disciplined and motivated towards his goal.

When asked what it might feel like to be a famous ballet dancer, he paused, as though he had not contemplated it before. The question wasn't seeking information about the applause, the opening nights and the pre-stage jitters, but rather the daily pressure of being as good as the reviews said you were the previous night. We talked about all the different aspects that being a famous ballet dancer might entail. William showed great resistance to actually picturing himself as famous and successful in his chosen field.

He needed the process to be broken down into small steps, to enable him to get used to the idea that he really might achieve fame and success. At this point he became impatient, telling me he didn't want to take many smaller steps. He simply wanted to be famous. William seemed afraid of all that was required to be famous and successful. When he sat down and thought about it, he felt overwhelmed.

If the whole process consisted of 100 steps, William had already taken about 55 or 60 of them. All he had to do was to train his expectations and beliefs about success with the same discipline that he had trained his body.

His parents were waiting for him to give up dancing and get a 'proper job'. He needed to increase his beliefs in the possibility of becoming famous and successful before he could comfortably achieve his goals, but he had already surrendered to the beliefs about life and success that he'd learned from his family. As yet, he had not challenged them.

After a few visits William discontinued his sessions. He seemed to be weighed down by parental expectations and his own growing impatience with the steps required to realise his goals. During the battle to conquer his core beliefs, he appeared to have lost the will to be a successful dancer.

If talent alone was able to guarantee success, William might have been a great dancer. However, persistence is usually an important ingredient in any successful career, and William lacked this vital quality.

The past can slow your progress with unresolved issues weighing heavily on your mind. Resolving issues from the past or simply laying them to rest can release you to pursue your purpose with less effort. Periodically it pays to review the past, to determine what has sharpened your perception and what is merely mental or emotional baggage.

The habits you have formed can bring you towards or away from your purpose. Establishing more productive habits consciously takes time and effort, but the rewards are worth the effort. When you next reflect on your past, notice those habits which have been useful and effective, along with those which are outdated now.

CHAPTER FIVE

The Power of the Present

Although you may not *like* your current path in life, it is familiar. There may be influences that make it either hard for you to change your course or that reward you for treading a beaten path.

Inertia needs to be examined as it can prevent you from taking that all-important first step towards a goal or your purpose. Inertia often conceals more complicated issues, including a fear of failure, or that success might require that you leave behind friends, family or a location forever.

Those who have achieved great success know that it comes with a price. If such success arrives too quickly, for instance, fear of change may drive you to avoid it in order to return to the safety of your familiar life.

Phillip was teaching his four-year-old grandson to count. Findbar was bored with the whole concept until Phillip offered him all the shiny (newly minted) coins in his wallet, telling him he could keep them if he counted them accurately. If not, they were to be returned to Phillip's wallet. Findbar became focused, careful and diligent as he arranged the twenty-cent pieces in groups of five to count them more easily. His desire for the money had overcome his boredom with numbers, for numbers were suddenly offering an opportunity for wealth.

Purpose often requires that you direct your thoughts, your attentions and your efforts toward a precise goal or direction, in order to conquer each step on the path to your goal. As we have already said, the pursuit of goals can demand sacrifices, effort and a sense of purpose. At these times, inertia is the part of us that suggests that it's all going to be wasted effort, and that the comfortable sofa is a good place to be.

Inertia keeps the way clear for those who want the goal badly enough. When you find your perfect port in life, it's unlikely to be crowded, because all those residing there have had to make at least the same effort as you to arrive there. Sometimes those around you who lack a sense of direction may resent the effort you put into achieving your own purpose. They may attempt to distract you from it in various ways.

When Cassie, a neighbour, has an important task to complete, and her daughter, Sarah, wants her attention, she tries distracting her mother through conversation. She begins with a question, or she may deliberately mispronounce something so that Cassie will tell her how it should be said. At this point she has her mother's complete attention. To prevent a mental tug of war, Cassie explains the important task she has to do and how long she expects it to take. She then asks Sarah what she'd like them to do together afterwards. Then they both have the same agenda: to have Cassie's goal achieved. When that happens, Cassie feels a sense of fulfilment, while her daughter has her full attention on something she likes to do.

Choosing to find and pursue your purpose or choosing to be distracted by all the shiny baubles life offers are simply that — choices. While they may appear hard decisions at first, the rewards soon indicate whether or not you have taken the right path.

CHAPTER SIX

Finding the Way

When many of us embark on the search for our true purpose, we usually begin by looking outwardly for signs. The task is simpler than that. The signs are not outside us, but within.

More often than not, **a part of us already knows or remembers our true purpose.** Instead of looking outside ourselves, we need only find that part which knows where we are meant to be heading. Distractions occur outside, whereas direction is often found within.

It is important to listen to our inner voice. Our physical bodies contain many of the answers. Often, however, we do not listen to our bodies in order to escape the feelings we have stored there. Yet unresolved grief, pain, anger or resentment has to be acknowledged before we can feel or notice more subtle things, such as purpose.

This is one of the reasons why ongoing counselling can be effective in helping you to restore your awareness of purpose. As you resolve the residual feelings from past incidents, it becomes easier for you to listen to your body. If you begin to experience good feelings, often the impressions relayed to your mind are more welcome. The habit of listening to your physical self can be established with patience and practice.

As you feel more alive, you are likely to notice your body more and to be aware of what it likes and dislikes. When you pay attention, your body alerts you to how it feels about people, situations and circumstances. Not listening to your body, in order to escape the negative feelings it contains, reduces a valuable source of information. It is possible to lose your way if you effectively cut yourself off from what you feel is right for you.

Paying attention to your body is one way of finding those things that fulfil you or give you purpose. Your body often reveals things it feels good about. Soon you can be experiencing the rich inner rewards associated with doing what you love to do.

Kyle arrived at a party looking dishevelled and feeling emotionally flat. His unkempt appearance suggested he'd only just awoken. In the course of a conversation, he revealed that playing the piano was one of the few things that had brought him happiness in his childhood.

Growing up in a family of five children, money had been tight and there wasn't a piano in his childhood home. Each Sunday, however, Kyle and his family visited a family that owned a piano, so each week Kyle used to play for a few hours.

The piano represented more than music to Kyle. Its clean keys and the fact that it was tuned to concert pitch represented perfection in a world filled with chaos. After sitting alone in the gracefully furnished music room playing that piano each Sunday, Kyle returned home to the squalid life of poverty, chaos, struggle and disharmony resulting from five people living in a very small flat.

Soon music, particularly pianos, came to represent a perfect, ordered universe to him. As he improved his skills at the piano, he grew confident that it was possible to contribute to a sense of order and harmony in his surroundings.

As an adult, Kyle became too busy to pursue the piano, and his skills diminished from a lack of practice. He was lacking a deep sense of his own purpose in life.

Kyle later approached a friend who had a piano, and he resumed playing. Within a month he'd arranged to have the piano tuned. He began to spend one afternoon a month cleaning and polishing it lovingly. With regular practice, his keyboard skills gradually returned.

Kyle had returned to one of the things that had given him fulfilment in the past. It still offered him fulfilment. This is not always the case, however. Sometimes things that once fulfilled us offer only a nostalgic experience when repeated.

Having found one thing in life that gave him a sense of peace and fulfilment, Kyle became determined to look for similar opportunities. He eventually purchased a piano for himself and took lessons, improving his skills as well as his sense of an order in the universe. As he pursued these need-fulfilling activities, many more needs surfaced. A part of him realised that his inner voice was able to be heard.

Depression and lack of purpose often mask the fact that we are denying our inner needs in the pursuit of other things, such as money and material comforts. While struggling to attain a comfortable life, we may devote most of our waking hours to activities we really don't like. As a result, in our spare time, we are often too tired or depleted to pursue those things that we find more fulfilling. It is important to recognise the full price we may be paying for the pursuit of comfort if we are drained to the core at the end of our working life. If you cram your life with unfulfilling pursuits, in retirement you are likely to harvest boredom.

Finding the part of us that knows our true purpose requires listening. It's not a simple process because we may first have to listen to all those resentments we have not expressed. We may also unearth dreams and hopes which need fulfilment.

After acknowledging losses and disappointments we have experienced, we can then become still enough to listen to that soft voice within which remembers our purpose. This may seem like a long way round to reaching something as simple and basic as purpose, but it is precisely what has been layered over it that prevents us from seeing it clearly.

If we fail to confront unresolved grief, loss, anger and resentment, we may stop searching for our purpose in a bid to avoid the pain we associate with it. Very few people can sit with the powerlessness that accompanies deep grief and loss for long periods of time. Sometimes it is important to revisit this pain periodically, until it has been dealt with thoroughly.

Rita's story is a clear example. Her childhood was like a war zone. Her father was a strict disciplinarian, to the point of madness. He regularly beat her and locked her in the garden shed overnight as punishment for perceived misdeeds. During those nights she slept huddled beneath hessian sacks, often disturbed by the strange sounds of the local wildlife. Eventually she managed to hide a small torch in the shed for emergencies.

Depression and lack of purpose often mask the fact that we are denying our inner needs in the pursuit of other things.

Rita wasn't in search of her life's purpose; she was in search of her life. As she ran her slender fingers through her strawberry blonde hair, she verbalised how unfair it was that she had experienced such a traumatic childhood. The nightmares still disrupted her sleep at least once a week.

As she worked through the resentment of her ill-treatment, Rita encountered grief for the loss of her childhood years. Over the months she revisited this pain, retreating whenever she felt herself becoming overwhelmed by it. Her nervous darting eyes betrayed a frightened girl within the woman Rita had become.

It was difficult for Rita to accept that she was not going to have her childhood again. She realised that if she wanted positive memories of the past, she'd have to experience good things now and recall them in the years to come. At that point in her life, she had very few positive experiences from her past.

Instead of returning to what had once brought her a sense of fulfilment, she had to search for entirely new things, things which carried no negative associations. Rita was encouraged to try at least four new experiences each month for one year. So, over the next year she attended courses, films, plays, sporting events, private lessons in writing, painting, astrology, singing, dancing, sailing, photography, cooking and clothes designing. She enrolled at a local gym, travelled to other cities to explore life as a tourist and took a language course.

At first she felt sick with fear at having to arrive at a class and face a group of strangers, until, after the third course, she realised that she didn't have to get to know any of them, and that she might not see them again once the course concluded. Soon she made a few friends from the classes she attended.

Rita was motivated to move forward into new experiences, despite her fear of meeting strangers, because, whenever she reviewed her past, she knew that she didn't want to continue living the life she had been living up to that point. Moving on wasn't easy. At times it depleted her emotionally and financially, but she desperately wanted new, positive memories to access. She pressed on with her commitment to try 50 new experiences in twelve months.

At the end of that year, Rita realised that she had made three new friends and five new acquaintances. She had discovered that although she didn't like writing, painting, photography or clothes design, she loved cooking, travelling, live theatre and archaeology.

How many of us have 50 new experiences each year as an adult? For young children, 50 new experiences each year is not uncommon, yet as adults, our routines, responsibilities and habits keep us to a limited repertoire. To determine how many new experiences you have encountered in the past twelve months, try the questionnaire below:

- How many new foods or flavours have you tasted in the last twelve months?

- How many articles of clothing have you purchased in new designs or colours during the last twelve months?

- How many people have you met in the last twelve months who weren't met in the course of business or career?

- How many new musical CDs, DVDs or videos have you viewed or listened to in the last twelve months?

- How many new films have you seen in the last twelve months?

- How many new books have you read in the last twelve months?

- Have you travelled to any new and unfamiliar destinations in the last twelve months?

- Have you moved house or changed your job in the last twelve months?

- If you haven't moved, have you redecorated your home in any way in the last twelve months?

- Have you attended any courses or workshops in the last twelve months?

- How many new friends or acquaintances have you made in the last twelve months?

- When offered a new experience, are you willing to jump in to see what it's like, or do you hold back from fear of failure?

You might have found that it's not that difficult to reach 50, but some people really do struggle to chalk up even one new experience a week.

If you're a struggler, you might ask yourself how you expect to find your purpose if you continue to do what you've always done, especially if you know that it is not leading you anywhere?

All new experiences are not necessarily risky, highly expensive or time-consuming. If you fear them, however, opportunities may become invisible to you.

Habits govern much of what we do in the course of a week. That is precisely why supermarkets periodically rearrange their stock on the shelves. They realise that with repeated visits, most customers see only those things they usually buy, and all the other items become invisible to them. By rearranging stock, they force customers to remain aware of what is actually on the shelves and perhaps discover something they have not previously purchased but which suits them.

It's not enough to realise that you are not experiencing many new things in your life. Sometimes it pays to consciously seek out opportunities for new experiences. This may include 'rearranging the supermarket shelves' in your life, in order to avoid blindly treading over and around the very opportunities for which you are searching.

Finding the way is easier if you realise that distractions occur outside and direction comes from within. Finding the way for you is possible if you:

- Listen to your physical body.

- Notice which experiences in your life your physical body reacts positively and negatively to.

- Remember that cramming your life with unfulfilling pursuits can lead to a harvest of boredom and regret.

- See what life can be like for you by trying new experiences.

- Bear in mind that what suits others may not suit you.

CHAPTER SEVEN

Changing Habits

Having identified where you are presently and where you want to go, you'll probably need to change some of your behaviour patterns in order to make the most of your life when it improves. Moreover, by observing your habits for a period of time, you'll know which ones you need to change in order to propel yourself towards your goals.

Jasmine wanted to become a writer and needed effective routines. As a mother of two children, aged five and seven, her days were full. At the end of each day, when the children were asleep, she was usually too tired to think clearly.

Jasmine decided that if she wanted time alone to write, undisturbed, she'd have to take it early in the morning, before the children awoke. This meant that she'd have to change her sleeping habits. She worked out that if she went to bed at 9 o'clock each weeknight, she'd be able to wake at 5:45 am and start writing at 6 am. This gave her 90 minutes of peace to think and write without interruption.

It took five weeks before Jasmine awoke naturally and adjusted to her new sleeping patterns. In those first weeks she stared at the computer screen, wrote email to friends and generally yawned her way through the 90 minutes. Her younger daughter, Dianne, discovered that if she woke early, she had her mother's complete attention, so Jasmine had to teach her not to disturb her before 7:30 am.

Through pure chance Jasmine commenced her new sleeping patterns in spring. It wasn't difficult to climb out of bed when the sun was rising. The same was true throughout summer. It became more arduous when winter arrived, but by that time, however, she had already established her new habits, which were not too difficult to maintain.

By the time winter arrived, Jasmine had written several short stories, one of which she had sold to a magazine. She was working on a short book when the cold, dark mornings of winter tempted her to stay in bed for another two hours every day. The success she already had behind her was enough motivation to keep her at it. By the second summer, she had sold four short stories and was close to completing the book.

Timing for commencing new habits is important. It's going to be more difficult giving up sweet foods at Christmas or to take up walking or swimming every day in the middle of winter. Once you have identified the new habits you want to establish, you need to decide whether you want to jump in and change them all at once, or ease into them one or two at a time.

Effective habits are better established at the same time. Virginia decided to reduce weight and to increase her fitness. She changed her diet and started attending yoga classes in the same week. Although it was hard at first, she found that as she reduced weight, her fitness levels improved. After hard work, focused thinking and commitment, she had the twin rewards of the figure she desired, and increased stamina and energy throughout the day.

Sometimes the timing for establishing new patterns of behaviour begins effectively, but life then gets in the way. An example of this was Kurt, who came to me to help him stop smoking. As a result of hypnosis, he was making progress over the first three weeks. He reduced his smoking without finding it too difficult, because of a simple, portable relaxation technique that he practised whenever the need arose.

Three weeks into the sessions (which usually take between four to six weeks), Kurt learned that redundancies were planned for his workplace within the month. At 45, he felt apprehensive about the chances of securing another position at senior level, were he to be retrenched. This was certainly a real test of his new relaxation technique. To ease into it, he chose to smoke as much as he needed, without judging himself, until the work situation had been resolved. He didn't want the additional stress of nicotine withdrawal during this already stressful period.

Kurt's hypnosis sessions were extended to cover the period until retrenchments were announced, so that he might have some support through those difficult weeks. He continued with the relaxation technique, especially as he now had two simple, portable ways to relax. He survived the retrenchments and gradually replaced smoking with his new relaxation technique. It had proven to be effective during the mounting tension he had experienced. He realised that as he became more familiar with the technique, it was more effective in relaxing him.

Sometimes you increase your chances of success in changing habits if you enlist the help of others, but be careful whom you ask. Ensure that those who assist you have nothing invested in your remaining the way you are. Experience with clients has shown that family members are not always the best people from whom to seek support when you want to change habits.

When you change your behaviour patterns, those around you may feel threatened or uncomfortable. Consciously or unconsciously, they may try to have you return to your old ways. When you have decided to reduce weight, your partner arrives home with a family-sized cheesecake and two bottles of red wine. When Dad wants to keep the car at home on Saturday so that he can wash it, son turns to sport on the TV, and Dad is soon settled in on the sofa, happy to lend the car to his son. Selecting someone who is unlikely to have anything invested in keeping you where you are in life can be a rewarding way to strengthen your chances of success.

Support groups can be helpful in ensuring that your new habits take hold. In regular meetings, others describe the very problems you are experiencing and how they effectively dealt with them. There can be a sense of camaraderie, and you often have more experienced role models to give you something tangible to aim for.

The buddy system works well, too. If you take up walking for an hour each day and you have a local friend who also walks, you can motivate each other. A third person increases your chances of success, for when one of you doesn't feel like walking on some particular day, the other two can still motivate each other.

This occurred with Claire, a mother of two school-aged children, who took up walking to reduce weight and increase fitness. She walked for an hour and a half each afternoon. Within five months, her friends noticed the difference. She was the shape she wanted to be, and also more positive in her approach to life generally. Her friend Pam joined her and together they walked each weekday, talking and laughing as they went. Soon they were joined by Tracey and Peter.

The time came when Claire was unable to walk every day. With her university exams approaching, she needed to spend more time at home studying, while the others continued as before. She complained to the others that she felt restless and that she missed her walks. Peter then came up with a plan to allow Claire to walk with them and still not miss out on her studies. She made a list of all the points she had to memorise, handed the sheets to Peter, and he tested her as they walked.

After completing her exams, Claire thanked Peter for all his help with a long lunch in a garden cafe which they passed during their daily walks. Facing one particularly difficult question in the exams, she had recalled how it had come up several times as they climbed the tallest hill on their walk. Recalling the hill, the walk and Peter's wording of the question, Claire had been able to recall the answer.

A counsellor or a life coach can be invaluable in helping you to establish new and more rewarding life patterns, as they are usually objective in their approach to your life goals. Sometimes they can point out that it is not one isolated issue, but instead, a pattern of behaviour that has resulted in the issue you are facing.

Rodney sought out a counsellor because he had fallen in love with his best friend's sister, Clara. Clara wasn't interested in a relationship with Rodney, although she enjoyed his company. The pain of being around someone who did not return his feelings soon sapped Rodney's confidence.

A counsellor or a life coach can be invaluable in helping you to establish new and more rewarding life patterns, as they are usually objective in their approach to your life goals.

His dreams at night were filled with images of Clara. Eventually he had to keep his distance from her, as he found being around her too painful. After three months of regular weekly counselling, Rodney realised that he had a pattern of falling in love with women who weren't interested in him. Those who did return his feelings soon held no attraction for him. His quest seemed to be to win the love of someone who at first showed no interest.

With the help of his counsellor, Rodney traced the pattern all the way back to his first love relationship — a classic case of unrequited love. The pattern was traced back still further, to his mother, who had been busy working hard while he was young, having limited time and energy for him. Now Rodney had several choices: blame his upbringing, his circumstances or fate for not sending him someone whose indifference turned to love, or change his behavioural patterns. Recognising the pain that lay ahead if he did not change, Rodney chose the latter option.

It took him two years and consistent support to change his relationship patterns, but the rewards included finding someone whom he loved and who also returned his feelings. Now five years later, Rodney says he still feels the occasional twinge when he meets an aloof woman, who appears immune to his charm. He has mentioned that he still feels the stirring of the old hopes: to be loved by someone who isn't interested at first. These feelings soon fade, however, as he reminds himself that it was this pattern of behaviour that had brought pain and offered no real rewards.

A coach or counsellor may also assist you in breaking down your goals into more manageable steps, which will allow you to pace yourself as you change habits and reassess your direction from time to time.

When large goals are broken down into a series of small steps, they are more achievable. Even short-term goals can be treated the same way. By listing each step, you can see where you are on the path to your goal at any time.

Kevin's preparation for his weekly four-hour radio program is a simple example. He usually begins mentally at his intended destination (the close of the program) and lists each step backwards. A recent list looked something like this:

- Say goodnight as I fade into the last track.

- Thank my guest for being a part of the program.

- Interview the guest.

- Play music and announce the imminent arrival of my guest musician for the evening.

- Telephone interview with a sportswoman.

- Check the play list and cue first song.

- Phone guest to confirm attendance and arrival time for the interview.

- Script notes for personal interview.

- Script questions for telephone interview.

Kevin begins with the last thing he expects to do and asks himself what is likely to come before that. When the list is complete, he reverses the order in which things appear, and thus has a detailed list of steps for the forthcoming program.

If you make a plan of many small steps towards a goal, keep the plan, even after you've realised your goal. It may serve to motivate you when another goal is desired. Whenever you're feeling overwhelmed, it can remind you of what is possible. At the risk of overstating this, almost anything is possible if the steps are small enough and carefully planned. If you have a reward (your goal), a starting point (where you are), some support (through friends, a counsellor, coach or support group), a clear plan, a list of sequential steps and flexibility when issues arise that you hadn't planned for — almost any goal can be realised.

As an example let's take the act of producing a CD. Karen had the desire to record her own CD (her goal), so she hired a recording studio and organised a few musician friends to help out with accompaniment. They arrived at Michael's house, where the studio was set up in a small cottage in his back garden, recorded late into the evening and then spent four days editing their efforts. Five weeks later, they sat together, listening to their first CD.

Put in a point format, Karen's CD recording efforts might look like this:

- PURPOSE: Increasing fulfilment by securing more professional work as a singer.

- GOAL: To produce a CD featuring her voice.

- STARTING POINT: Selecting the songs and securing quotes for hire of studios for recording time.

- **SUPPORT:** Fellow musicians, friends, the recording engineer.

- **A CLEAR PLAN:** Arranging copyright permission for the songs to be used, organising suitable and available musicians, finding a recording studio, raising the necessary funds to finance the project, getting a quote for pressing the CD after editing, practising the songs with the musicians until they are of recording standard.

- **RESULT:** One CD to send to venues when approaching them for a paid live performance.

YOUR LIST:

PURPOSE:

GOAL:

STARTING POINT:

SUPPORT:

THE PLAN:

CHAPTER EIGHT

Checking Your Progress Regularly

Many people fail in the pursuit of their goals because, despite commencing with great plans, they fail to check their progress regularly. The more regularly you check your steps against your plan, the quicker you can realise when you are off course and correct it.

If you have been off course for several weeks or months, it requires more effort to get back than if you have only been off course for a day or two. This was the case with Amelia, who didn't have a clue as to her purpose or even to a suitable career direction. Amelia was depressed and frustrated at her lack of career success but when questioned, she didn't know what she wanted to pursue as a career. Being somewhat shy and unassertive, she had drifted into administrative work but it was not fulfilling for her. When Amelia sat and reviewed her progress, her sense of frustration increased. This frustration was beneficial as Amelia was able to use it to motivate her to retrace her steps, to see when she was last fulfilled with her job and with her life.

It took repeated reviews before Amelia voiced that she had desired to pursue a career which involved helping others through healing or counselling when she left school. Instead, however, she succumbed to her parents, who pushed her into an administrative position because they thought it a safe option. Because Amelia had taken a path she hadn't wanted to take 15 years previously, it took longer for her to identify and to return to a suitable career path than had she made these changes only a year before.

Taking your eyes off the goal or the steps can result in disappointment. Modern society has made the pursuit of smaller goals so easy that many of us lack discipline when pursuing larger, more complicated goals.

As we become more reliant upon instant results, prolonging rewards until after the effort has been made can seem frustrating. Credit cards were probably invented with this impatience in mind. You can have it all now and pay for it later. The problems arise when you are working late to pay for something that is already worn out or, perhaps you're still paying for a holiday you took last year.

If you try to change your life direction and establish new habits, it may feel strange, even uncomfortable, at first. In the same way that you would probably check a street directory several times when approaching an unfamiliar destination, you need to check your list of steps, to ensure you are progressing towards your desired goal.

One difficulty with larger goals is that you may need to take steps away from it before proceeding towards it. Janice wanted to open her own business, but she had debts and had to repay these and control her expenses before she could start a business. An enthusiastic and restless person, Janice wanted the instant solution. (Just add water and boil for five minutes.) As we discussed her business goals she squirmed and fidgeted with her pen, her rings and her hair, twirling it around in her fingers absentmindedly. Her mannerisms suggested that if even small tangible results weren't immediately forthcoming, she'd abandon our sessions in favour of a more radical approach. This meant several plans:

- PLAN 1: Decreasing her current expenses.

- PLAN 2: Increasing her income (by a second job) in order to repay her debts more rapidly.

- **PLAN 3:** Saving seed money for her new business.

- **PLAN 4:** Studying small business management through courses and reading, and eventually working part-time in a small business.

For months Janice worked very hard, yet she felt that her goal of owning her own business was slipping further away from her. In reality, she was learning how to control her expenses, something that all small business owners need to know if they want to remain solvent. She grew weary with all the extra effort required at her second job, and despondent when she noticed how much extra tax she was paying by working two jobs. Janice realised that these frustrations were important steps, as they'd serve as a reminder of what she might expect if she didn't control her expenses when she was running her own business. She also realised that earlier on, in formulating her goals, she had been less than realistic.

She had dreamed of spending $30,000 or more decorating a small shop, with trips overseas to buy beautiful stock items. After working two jobs for six months to repay her existing debts, she revised her plan, deciding to spend only up to $2000 to set up her business, and sourcing most of her stock through local importers or the Internet.

Each time she felt trapped in her life and overwhelmed with her debts, Janice had previously responded by spending on her credit cards. At her current rate of 'rewarding herself' via credit card spending, she was likely to still be saving for business seed money in five years. She really needed to look at the hard facts. Most people cannot survive in a small business. Few people have the necessary skills, discipline, small business education, marketing experience, ability to research their customers' needs and ongoing dedication and energy to make a small business survive beyond five years.

Janice decided that it was a long-term project, and she'd learn as much as possible before taking the step of signing a lease for premises. This learning was likely to include self-discipline in spending, finding alternatives for rewarding herself when she felt trapped and consulting with those who were best able to advise her regarding her business. It took six weeks for Janice to decrease her expenses and adjust accordingly. She cut up all but one of her credit cards and used the local gym to reduce the feelings of being trapped by debt and work. It took another 24 months for her to repay her debts and six more months to save enough to start her business.

During this last six months, she undertook a course in small business management. Throughout the process she read several books on the joys and pitfalls of small business management. When she was ready to locate suitable premises for her shop, Janice was debt-free. She had saved enough to get her through the first four months of trading.

Janice met Sandy on the small business management course and they started a business together. With Sandy's savings added to Janice's, they had enough to get them through the first six months of trading and to comfortably stock the shop. The business has been running successfully for 20 months now, but the steps aren't over yet. Janice has new goals, which involve expanding to include the shop next door and beginning a mail and Internet order service. Because she has successfully proven herself by taking the previous steps, there is a good chance she'll realise her new goals.

Janice is committed to checking her progress on a weekly basis, reviewing each step taken and refining the path to her goals. Aside from the weekly meetings with Sandy and the monthly sessions with her accountant, she consults regularly with a business adviser, to ensure that she remains focused. From time to time she had complained that the consultant's and the accountant's fees were too big an expense, and that she'd be better off putting that money towards new stock. She had reduced the frequency of the sessions with her business adviser and her accountant. After three months, it had become apparent to her that her focus was slipping away from her goal. Returning to the previous schedule for the sessions with her advisers resulted in a strengthening of her focus once again.

Wanting a goal is not a guarantee that you have the necessary discipline to reach it or maintain it. Years ago a friend took private lessons in ice-skating. Anne's teacher was experienced with students who had high hopes but lacked discipline, so she had a rule for payment. All private lessons were to be paid for in advance, three lessons ahead. If a student missed a lesson, it was already paid for. This policy had the effect of making Anne and the other students get out of bed on cold mornings and drive to their lessons, despite longing to sleep in late.

Below are listed some ways that you can review your progress. It is essential that you do so regularly — as often as you can. Reviewing your goals and maintaining the excitement is necessary to motivate you to achieve them. This enthusiasm may be effectively channelled into the steps you are taking, making them seem easier to accomplish.

Wanting a goal is not a guarantee that you have the necessary discipline to reach it or maintain it.

There are several ways to keep the dream alive, to maintain the initial excitement. One of the most effective is to anchor the realisation of your goal in the senses. If the goal is a new car, take a ride in the model you will eventually have, feeling the seats, smelling the interior. Keep photographs or brochures of your physical goals, or of those things you'll do when you have realised intangible goals. When Trevor decided to reduce weight and build muscle, he cut out a photo of a lean, well-built man and stuck it to the refrigerator door. A week later he found an old photo of himself and transposed the photo of his head onto the figure on the fridge. Every day he saw this image, reminding him of his goal. Meanwhile, his fitness trainer at the local gym kept a detailed record of each step of Trevor's progress, motivating him towards his goal.

Another way to keep your dreams alive is to mix with people who have already achieved what you want. If you are building an investment portfolio, then attend some stockholders' meetings and mix with those who are already successful investors.

Your goal is likely to have a feeling, a smell, perhaps even a sound to it. These can act as reminders to sharpen your focus. When Roberta set her goal as first place in the national showjumping competition, she purchased some blue ribbon and had a friend photograph her in her full outfit with her horse. She had the photograph enlarged and placed it on her bedroom wall. Each morning she awoke to her toothy grin staring down at her. When glimpsing the photo for the first time her father asked, 'So tell me; which one is the horse again?' She punched him lightly on the arm and promptly bet him one year's agistment fees if she won first place in a showjumping competition within two years. This was the image she saw first thing in the morning and last thing at night. Soon she was dreaming of blue winners' ribbons at night. This motivated her to practise diligently in order to improve her show-jumping skills. Two years later after strenuous work Roberta finally had her winning ribbon. She replaced the old photograph with a poster-sized one of the genuine ribbon, and reminded her father of their bet.

Keeping accurate records of past success in the pursuit of goals can also act as a motivator. When Clara felt dejected at not being able to change jobs to something more rewarding, she consulted her resumé, which surprised her. Positive references from past employers were a written reminder of her skills and personal qualities.

To review your goals:

- Keep a daily diary. This helps you to notice your positive and negative habits.

- Keep a chart or a visual reminder of how far you have come towards your goal.

- Consult a counsellor or experienced coach on a regular basis. This helps you to receive positive feedback on the steps taken and encouragement when you feel overwhelmed.

- Take some photographs of each important step on the way to your goal. For example, if you are building muscle or reducing weight, it may motivate you to have a series of photographs of yourself at each step. Being able to glimpse the real differences as the steps unfold can inspire you to continue. If you are paying off debts, then striking off each one from a list or crossing off an image representing each debt as it is repaid is a reminder of the rewards of your efforts.

- Talk about your progress with a support group.

- Discuss your past and present steps with a friend who is pursuing a similar goal.

- Set aside time at regular intervals (perhaps at the beginning of each month) to review your goal, the steps already taken and the ones still to come. Give yourself a small reward every time you review your process, to build a positive association with the review process.

- Be inventive. Jason felt that he was becoming obsessively competitive and to prevent this occurring he had a large trophy made up with an engraving that read: 'To our fabulous friend Jason, from all of us here in heaven.' He placed it on the mantle among his sailing trophies to remind him of the bigger picture. Although each sailing competition was important to him, he realised that life is bigger than sailing.

After you have identified your goal, it pays to review your progress regularly in order to prevent yourself straying too far from the path. Just as you might check your progress when following a recipe or assembling a piece of furniture which arrives in kit form, reviewing your progress in life is essential for success.

CHAPTER NINE

Personal Fulfilment

If you're going to live for 60 or 70 years, you may as well make the effort worthwhile. Make the ride enjoyable.

If you were planning a long drive across country, you would probably take a few necessities with you, including tools, food, water, music, and a jacket in case of a cold snap. You might also ask someone to accompany you. Planning the journey increases the probability that it will be enjoyable.

If you set off on your trip without any thought of your hunger or thirst, stopping for food and drink on the way, you can still enjoy the journey. Before you commence the return trip, experience may encourage you to reconsider your needs.

On life's journey, you have probably travelled far enough to know what to expect of the road ahead. On the following pages are some tools for ensuring that the remainder of your journey is worthwhile.

How good your start in life was, and how hard it has been for you to make it this far, are not the most important considerations. Personal fulfilment is about making the rest of your journey worthwhile for you.

Some people pack the car to the roof with items for any possible situation prior to a trip. They probably require a great many things to feel fulfilled. Others throw a few things onto the back seat and set off, confident that they can pick up anything they need along the way.

Different approaches suit different people, but if the journey is to be enjoyable and successful, you may benefit from some planning. There is no point in setting a goal that is going to make you miserable. Personal fulfilment is as essential in goal-setting as it is in life purpose. It may seem a long way off in some periods, but a strong sense of your life's purpose usually gets you through those times.

Personal fulfilment was sporadic for Quentin, who found scant demand for his musical act in clubs and hotels. To cheer him up, his friend and fellow musician Ferdi asked Quentin to accompany him for a drink in a city hotel. As they were leaving home, Ferdi suggested that they each bring an instrument. After a few schooners, they strolled along the quayside amidst a throng of tourists. Producing his guitar, Ferdi began singing. Quentin joined in with his flute, and a crowd gathered. The guitar case eventually glittered with gold coins as the two friends fulfilled themselves through song.

After three hours of playing favourites, improvising and taking requests, Quentin and Ferdi ate heartily in a nearby restaurant. They counted their earnings, laughing over a bottle of wine at how they had stumbled through a few songs. Buoyed by their initial success, they played along the quayside throughout the summer. What had started out as a way to cheer Quentin up turned out to be a source of financial and creative fulfilment for several months. The following summer, they repeated their success.

Quentin's purpose was to entertain others, primarily through music. Initially unable to generate an income by playing in a bar or a club, he found a more suitable venue without the smoke and the tables of patrons ignoring him. An opportunity for short-term fulfilment provided a longer-term outlet for Quentin's creativity.

Without breaking personal fulfilment down into its smallest components, you may agree that it is composed mainly of the following areas:

- HEALTH — vitality

- RELATIONSHIPS (INCLUDING FRIENDSHIPS) — intimacy and honesty

- HOME ENVIRONMENT — a place to be yourself

- FAMILY — like-minded people

- CAREER — meaningful work.

Finding the right combination of the above areas can mean the difference between fulfilment and frustration.

PERSONAL FULFILMENT EXERCISE

Using a scale of 1 to 100 (number 1 being disenchantment and 100 being total fulfilment) complete the rating exercise below:

- How do you rate your personal fulfilment over the last year? Taking the case of Quentin (above), a complete lack of personal fulfilment might be not having a musical instrument, or not being able to entertain an audience with it. Complete fulfilment might be the applause from a large and enthusiastic audience at a well-paid venue, where he performs his own compositions and later signs copies of his latest CD.

- On the same scale, how do you rate your personal fulfilment on average for the past five years?

- What levels of fulfilment do you realistically expect from life over the coming year?

- What levels of fulfilment do you realistically expect from life over the next five years?

- What is the single most important action you can take to ensure a greater personal fulfilment over the next five years? If you are an artist, do you need to attend more classes? If you're ambitious to further your career, do you need to gain more credentials?

Making your life's journey worthwhile requires effort at first, until the new patterns of behaviour become habits. A small example of this occurred with Hank a few years ago. He often found that when he was ready to leave the house, he couldn't find his keys. It was comical watching him go through his routine. He'd ask everyone if they'd seen his keys. Then he'd overturn every cushion, book, newspaper and ornament in the house before checking his car to see that he hadn't locked them in the vehicle. At this point he was usually swearing and blaming everyone from the dog through to his ex-wife, who lived interstate. After many frustrating minutes spent searching all over, he'd finally discover them and storm out the front door. It occurred to him one day that the simplest solution was to leave his keys in the same place every time he came home.

It took Hank around four months to make this a habit. Now he rarely has to hunt for the keys. If he was able to do that for a set of keys, what else might he change by establishing new habits?

The acquisition of new habits can mean that you grow and maintain a garden, run a business more effectively, save money or improve your diet. Each new habit requires effort at first, and yet each eventually becomes a natural, rewarding routine.

Before you can replace your current habits or behaviour patterns, you need to know what it is that you want. Try the following exercise:

PERSONAL FULFILMENT EXERCISE

- What **physical** pursuits do you expect will give you a greater sense of fulfilment over the next five years? These might include travelling, achieving your sports aims or health and fitness goals, or building a home.

- What **emotional** goals do you expect will give you a greater sense of fulfilment over the next five years? These may include a new love relationship, healing a past relationship or friendship or finding new ways to fulfil yourself emotionally.

- What **mental** objectives do you expect will give you a greater sense of fulfilment over the next five years? These may include learning new skills, mastering another language, finding a new personal philosophy or examining alternative ways of thinking.

- What **spiritual** accomplishments do you expect will give you a greater sense of fulfilment over the next five years? These may include strengthening your spiritual awareness and direction, examining spiritual alternatives or awakening to your spiritual purpose in life.

Why five years? Because too often, when we plan for fulfilment, we want instant results. Real change requires the establishment of new habits. Changing one habit can be a short process, but changing several takes time.

Public speaking is often listed as one of the most stressful situations to be confronted with. With practice, support and perseverance, it can become simply another routine. How many of us, however, actually make the effort to ensure that it does? Many avoid it, fear it and dread the moment we have to get up before an audience. Avoidance, fear and dread all require energy, perhaps not as much energy as changing our negative thoughts about public speaking, but energy nonetheless.

Now let's examine the four aspects of the personal fulfilment (previous) exercise, beginning with the physical accomplishments that might be expected to increase fulfilment. One client, Rudy, said that his desire to plant a garden was paramount. He had lived in various flats and houses for over 20 years. He longed for the day when he might plant a garden of his own, using his preferred trees, plants and design.

Rudy worked hard at clearing away overgrown shrubs. He read up on planting an organic garden (his new habit) to familiarise himself with the process. Within the twelve-month target period, he had cleared the space and prepared the soil for planting. Over the next six months, he planted and transplanted his garden until it had the shape he desired.

Is there any point in looking at material or physical goals to fulfil you if they offer no emotional fulfilment? In Rudy's case, he experienced a great deal of emotional fulfilment, derived initially from the simple act of planting his favourite plants and anticipating their warm colours in the seasons to follow. Hours flew past while Rudy tenderly nurtured his seedlings. He felt proud as he watched them grow and blossom. As the garden matured, he held garden parties. His guests gathered amongst the vibrant colours and the rich, heady scents that drifted across the well-manicured lawns.

Mental fulfilment includes learning new things, increasing your knowledge or understanding of a person (including yourself) or a situation. It can also include humour, taking courses in subjects that fascinate you, or studying to improve your career prospects.

For some, mental fulfilment comes from understanding an issue or a problem they've had to face. When grasping how they can better deal with such matters in the future, they feel mentally stretched.

Mental fulfilment can derive from reading, watching documentary films, or learning from those situations in which you find yourself. In Rudy's case it came from carefully planning a garden that offered something colourful every month of the year. From the daffodils and bluebells in early spring to the azaleas a month or two later and then the cosmos, sunflowers and lavender in summer, the various parts of the garden delighted him as they took turns to bloom.

There is no point in looking at material or physical things to fulfil you if there is to be no emotional fulfilment.

Feeding your spirit is as important as feeding your physical body. What feeds your spirit? Do you know how to increase your spiritual fulfilment in the coming years? An example of feeding the spirit was Thomas, a chiropractor. While some chiropractors may see their job as returning a physical body to a healthy alignment, Thomas perceives his task as restoring harmony to both the body and the spirit of each client.

He lovingly teaches chiropractic students about the joys of restoring humans to physical and spiritual health and vitality. He is centred, patient and focused in his work and, as a result, his reputation is spreading rapidly. Thomas feeds his spirit through meaningful work, knowing that his efforts bring joy to those who seek his talents.

Once you have mastered the basic skills necessary to pursue your purpose, it is likely to be a rewarding process. Expect fulfilment, joy, excitement and to be passionate about your path for this is life's way of tempting you towards the life which awaits you.

Allowing petty issues to distract you from your purpose lessens your sense of fulfilment. Your levels of fulfilment can act as a gauge to how closely you are following and fulfilling your purpose.

It is important that you seek and find fulfilment on all levels (physical, emotional, mental and spiritual) for prolonged hunger in any of these areas is likely to lead you away from your path, resulting in emptiness or an insatiable hunger within.

CHAPTER TEN

Meaningful Work

People working at something they love often radiate joy or enthusiasm. 'Work is love made visible,' states Kahlil Gibran in his book *The Prophet*. This is easily seen with classic sculptures, famous paintings and melodious music, but how about in the construction of a bridge or a railway tunnel?

We deserve to have meaningful work to sustain us. We have to find meaning in the work we do. Not all of us will be saving lives on a daily basis, breaking world records for endurance or making an immediate difference to the lives of those around us through our work.

Sometimes we have to step back from our daily work to see what it is offering us. Does it strengthen you by giving you responsibilities? Does it teach you the benefits of negotiating to have your needs met? In the simplest way, your work can be meaningful because it supports you and those close to you.

In a week of 168 hours, many of us are working longer than ever before. (So much for the increased leisure the new millennium was supposed to bring us!) This leisure time is probably out there in another dimension, along with the paperless office ... It is likely that the more time you put into a job, the less enjoyment you'll derive from it, simply due to needing some variety. Even too much of a good experience can reduce the joy of that experience. As businesses reduce staff and increase each employee's workload, it's natural that fulfilment levels fall, yet it doesn't have to be this way.

A friend, Renaldo, is a painter. Having raised his family, he decided to simplify his life in order to earn his living from what he loved to do — paint. After an amicable separation from his wife, they sold the family home, and Renaldo decided to move away from Sydney to somewhere less expensive.

For the first year he rented a small, rambling cottage and began improving his painting technique. In those twelve months, he was surprised at what he found he was able to live without. He managed without the expensive car, the nice clothes and the sumptuous dinners at local restaurants. But he also discovered what he couldn't live without, which included friends, good local beaches and access to entertainment. After twelve months, Renaldo moved again, settling close to a glorious beach. It took three years to finetune his lifestyle, but the efforts were worth the outcome. He now earns his living doing what he loves to do — painting. Because his outgoings are less than when he lived in Sydney, it is easier for him to manage.

This is not always the case, however. Circumstances were different for Claudette. She separated from her husband, and he moved out of the family home. She had a fourteen-year-old son and a twelve-year-old daughter, both of whom remained at home with her. Claudette's husband left her with a good home without a mortgage, and he pays her over $50,000 per year to cover her family expenses. Yet she complained to me that it simply wasn't enough. With the children's piano lessons, private school fees, upkeep on the car, rates, taxes and food, she was struggling. She commenced working part-time, but taxes ate most of her earnings. Two years later, she launched her own business from home. This helped to improve things slightly, but still she struggled.

At first I puzzled over why Renaldo was able to simplify his life, while Claudette could not. The children were a factor, but there were other reasons. Claudette felt compelled to continue the lifestyle to which she had been accustomed, and to continue to live as she did when her husband was with her. The choice was hers to make. Where children are concerned, parents usually want to give them the best possible start in life. Claudette was able to find meaningful work by starting her own business at home, although this took considerable time to eventuate.

Renaldo took over three years to establish the career that was meaningful to him, and pursuing his goal required effort and sacrifices. What is meaningful work to you? Try the meaningful work questionnaire below:

MEANINGFUL WORK QUESTIONNAIRE

- DO YOU NEED TO MAKE A DIFFERENCE TO THE WORLD AT LARGE?
  Some need to make a difference to many people, and fame is an essential part of their need for fulfilment.

- DO YOU NEED TO MAKE A DIFFERENCE TO THOSE CLOSE TO YOU IN YOUR DAILY LIFE?
  Others are not concerned with the world at large, preferring to avoid the public in favour of a smaller, more intimate environment. These people need to see results that are close to home for their efforts.

- DO YOU NEED TO HAVE A CLEARLY DEFINED GOAL TO PURSUE (A CAREER OR OTHER), IN ORDER TO HAVE A SHORT-TERM SENSE OF PURPOSE? For example, sales targets or production goals.
  Are you someone who doesn't feel as if you've achieved much until you've set and met a clear target? Do you like the feeling of doing rather than reflecting?

- IS IT IMPORTANT TO YOU TO WORK WELL WITHIN A TEAM?
  Do you enjoy teamwork and the results that can be achieved when a group of people work together on a project or towards

a goal? Well-balanced teams can often achieve more than an individual. Shared rewards can also unite the team. However, there can be drawbacks such as rivalry between team members.

- IS IT IMPORTANT TO YOU TO ENJOY INDEPENDENCE IN YOUR CAREER?
  Do you prefer to avoid teams in favour of the freedom that accompanies independence? Working alone allows you to set your own pace, but it often requires more self-discipline than teamwork.

Jane and Tristan provide an example of the difference between the first and second questions. Jane seeks a career in which she can make a difference to a large number of people at once. This has involved developing improved infrastructure in Third World countries. She seeks to make a difference to the world at large.

Tristan, on the other hand, prefers to work with clients on a one-to-one basis to change their lives, as he enjoys assisting one person at a time. He prefers to make a difference to those with whom his daily work brings him in direct contact.

Jane argues that the world will be a better place on a daily basis when everyone can have safe drinking water and electricity, and not run a daily risk of infection from pollution or inadequate sewerage. Tristan agrees with her, but is not inclined to battle through the bureaucratic jungle for years at a time to improve the lives of people he'll never see face to face. He argues that in his work as a psychologist he helps people resolve their emotional issues, allowing them to be more at peace with themselves and their world. In this way, the world becomes a better place because, one by one, more people are dealing with their personal issues, realising their potential in this lifetime. The basic difference is that Tristan can often see the changes he's helped to bring about with his clients. Jane has to trust that all of her efforts are not in vain, and that some bureaucrat or politician, for personal or cost-cutting reasons, doesn't undo five years of work.

Some people devote years at a time, overcoming overwhelming odds, to make the lives of others more rewarding. It can be through a grand career or in more simple and direct ways.

Recently an elderly man ordered a sandwich at a local lunch shop. The woman serving him obviously loved her work. She was cheerily chatting away to the regulars and to the other two sandwich-makers when she stopped and turned to him.

'You know what goes well with this?' she asked.

'Er, no. What?'

'Mayonnaise with finely chopped parsley,' she said, and he nodded, ready to give it a try.

Whether your work involves feeding people, entertaining them, supplying their cooking utensils or burying them, it can be meaningful to you. When work is looked on as meaningful, it is usually done with pride and perhaps also with flair. Anyone who has ever received bad service from a waiter or waitress in a restaurant knows what it is like to watch someone who doesn't see value in what they're doing.

Taking the steps to move from where you are presently towards work that you hope you will find meaningful can involve a long and arduous path, but if you don't do it, someone else may end up doing the job you want. Will they do it as well as you? Will they enjoy it as you hoped to?

Doing half a job or just enough work to 'get by' means that you are taking the easy way out. Too many people do that, and they offer no real competition to those who are focused and committed.

Josephine wanted to purchase a small house as an investment, so she visited a mortgage broker to arrange a loan. The woman who owned the franchise sat with her, explaining the procedure. She gave the impression of being knowledgeable, efficient and committed to Josephine's goal. Yet, a week later, she phoned back to say that she was unable to secure the funds Josephine required, and suggested she try again in a year or so.

Josephine promptly went out and applied at a local bank, securing the loan she wanted. It then occurred to her that as a mortgage broker, the woman she had consulted wasn't very good. How bad at your job do you have to be when a complete novice beats you to the finish line? Josephine was tempted to put her head into the mortgage broker's office to ask her if she had considered another line of work.

If you are devoting ten years of your life to a career or to a series of careers, you may as well make them rewarding.

Finding work that is meaningful to you is not easy, but consider that even if you work only 40 hours a week, for 48 weeks a year, and you work for 35 years, you'll have worked 56,000 hours. That's more than 333 weeks, 6.4 years of your life!

If you are one of those who work 50 to 70 hours per week, from age 25 until 65, the figure increases dramatically. At 50 hours per week, it jumps to 96,000 hours, or 10.9 years of your life.

Truly worthwhile and even amazing things can be achieved with ten years of your life. With 56,000 hours of training and direct experience, you can become a great psychologist, a fantastic baker, a well-respected gardener, a contented small business owner, an accurate editor or an enviable plumber.

As a customer, when you are parting with your hard-earned money for advice from a lawyer, you want the best, most committed lawyer your money can buy. You want someone who loves his or her work. You want someone who is happy to be a lawyer, because this person is more likely to be attentive to the task.

If you have no idea to what career you are suited, then perhaps it's time to seek advice. The quickest results can be found on the Internet, where some job websites offer a simplified version of the *Myers Briggs Type Indicator®* test to help you determine your personality type. The full test is available through career guidance counsellors, some psychologists and some job placement agencies.

More in-depth testing is offered by careers counsellors and the larger job agencies, usually for a fee. The fee is worth it if you are completely unsure about what might prove to be meaningful work to you. The next step may be to examine the study options, the training for the career you desire. A further step might be to see a life coach.

A sports coach can bring out the best in a sportsperson, and a good life coach can encourage the best in you for your life, addressing your issues, helping you to plan the path to your goals and breaking the steps down into manageable portions to encourage confidence in your abilities.

Coaches don't have to be professional psychologists or registered life coaches. Sometimes a good friend is all you need to help you clarify your life or your career direction. Vanessa typifies this style of a coach. As a teacher, she is used to solving problems, planning ahead her lessons, her school term and the whole school year, and simplifying issues to get results. When Zoltan has problems with his career, he consults Vanessa, and they talk. She encourages him to keep going and soothes him when he is frustrated with his work colleagues. After an hour or two, he feels inspired once again to strive for his career goals. Although it has none of the formality of a coaching session, it is coaching nonetheless.

When huge projects are broken down into smaller, more manageable sections, you can take small steps and eventually achieve big things.

For those who feel overwhelmed by the task ahead, perhaps it can be summarised this way:

- Find a personality test on the Internet. Alternatively, you might consult an experienced palmist for career guidance. This is a method that has been employed for hundreds of years.

- Complete the test and examine the results. Usually jobs are listed for each personality type.

- Alternatively, locate a careers guidance agency/counsellor close to you, and make an appointment for an aptitude test.

- Identify the types of careers that might suit you. If you have already done this, skip the next point.

- Find out what training is required for the job that appeals. See if you can be included for a week or two of unpaid work experience. Reading about a job and doing it are completely different.

- Train for your chosen career. If you are already in that career, examine your options for improving job satisfaction.

- Be sure to reward yourself regularly if you are pursuing long-term study or training, in order to keep yourself on track to your goal.

- Getting your dream job is not always enough. Sometimes you have to find your perfect place within the industry.

If you need two part-time jobs or two different types of work, perhaps having your own business may suit you. Some people cannot work at the same job for five days running, preferring a mix of tasks. Perhaps you might enjoy working in several locations on different days, or travel interstate or overseas with your work.

- Remember that your work is only a part of your life. Your purpose extends beyond how you earn a living, to encompass your friendships, your family, your home and your spiritual pursuits.

If you are devoting ten years of your life to a career or to a series of careers, you may as well make them rewarding. Of course, financial rewards are only one type of reward. Finding meaning is possible if you choose carefully.

How you spend your day is a choice. We've all heard people explaining why they have to do a certain type of work they dislike but, ultimately, it is a choice. Your alternatives may be bleak or non-existent where you presently live, but it is still a choice to remain there and pursue your career.

An example of this was a client who many years ago consulted me for help in changing her life direction. She had been working as a prostitute for three years, and she wanted to give it up.

Sally described the work as demeaning, demoralising and sometimes downright dangerous. When I asked her how she had started in prostitution, she explained that she had needed $3000 in a hurry. She had owed money all over the place, and creditors had started leaning on her for repayment. When I asked her if she had repaid the money, she replied that she had. She told me that she didn't owe anyone money now and that she'd purchased furniture, a car, clothes, a television and stereo in the time she'd been working in this field.

Over the weeks we discussed her interests, and the jobs she'd had prior to her current one. She didn't want to return to office administration, to being a personal assistant or to retail sales. During her brief stint as a tour guide, she had fallen overboard as the boat lurched off during an afternoon sightseeing cruise.

Sally was intelligent, quick-minded, articulate and resourceful. After some time, it seemed clear that she really didn't want to give up prostitution. It was the money.

'Where else can I earn $2500 for a few days' work?' she asked me when I suggested that she wanted to stay in the job. 'I can earn in three days what my fellow office workers earn in a month. And then I can have 27 days off on the beach if I want,' she added, adamant that she wasn't going back to office work.

'Do you take 27 days off and spend them on the beach?'

'No.'

'Why not?'

'Because I usually need more money, so I phone up and get a shift or two. Just enough to get me through, and then I take another week off.'

'Why?

'I'm spending more money than I used to.'

'Why?'

'Because I have more time to shop than before.'

'So, instead of spending 27 days on the beach, are you spending several hours in shops, until you are forced back to work?'

'Yes, something like that.'

'Is it possible that you are trapped in prostitution by your undisciplined spending?'

'Yes. Yes, I am.'

Knowing what you want to do is the first step.

It's likely that when you exercise little or no discipline in earning money, you exercise the same amount of discipline when spending it. Sally consulted me to help her leave a job she didn't like, but she lacked self-discipline, which made her task much more difficult.

In Sally's mind, all other work was underpaid and involved long hours. I wonder if she still believes that when she pays for her next dental appointment, or when she attends her next concert. Knowing what you want to do is the first step. Doing it successfully requires many more steps, which we'll examine in the following chapters.

CHAPTER ELEVEN

Rewarding Relationships

Chances are that while you pursue your life's purpose, someone you love is standing beside you — if not for the whole journey, then for a part of it. Appreciate this person and their support.

If you ignore your partner while you pursue your purpose, she or he will probably end up not being a part of either your purpose or your journey. On the other hand, clinging too tightly to partners probably means that they are not free to pursue their own purpose. If you prevent the one you love from doing that, you have made him or her your prisoner. Is that love?

Too often we see a man working so hard to provide for his family that he alienates them. Some children grow up rarely seeing the man of the house in the house because he's almost always working. When he is at home, he is tired or cranky from working too hard. Or he may be home because he is too ill to go to work.

Time spent with your children cannot be replicated, as they are continually growing and developing. The things they love one day may generate no interest a month later, for they have matured a bit more or entered another stage of development.

It seems that parents exert less and less influence over their children with the passing generations as less time is spent with the family. Those who spend the most time with you will influence you the most. It's similar to that old saying, 'If you want to control the direction of the company you work for, attend all the meetings'.

Is your relationship partner a part of your purpose? Does he or she support you towards it? Do you sideline him or her as you pursue your own plans? Do you secretly cherish a goal that does not include your partner?

This was the case with Gordon, whose plans for a leisurely retirement by the sea did not include his wife, Avril. Over a period of nearly 20 years, Gordon refused to take a holiday, preferring to scrimp and save for his personal goal in a secret offshore bank account. He purchased a small cottage that faced out to sea and was about to tell his unsuspecting wife of his plan to leave her when he was hospitalised with kidney pains. After three days of tests, Gordon died, leaving a letter that explained what he had planned.

Avril was overwhelmed by losing her life partner and shocked by the letter. At first she refused to believe it, until her lawyer confirmed that Gordon had used him to finalise the house purchase. When she had got over her shock and grief, Avril re-married and now lives happily in the cottage Gordon had purchased for himself. She also takes an extended holiday each year to redress the lack of holidays in years past.

Do you know what your partner's purpose is? Do you support him or her in the pursuit of that purpose? Are you included in it, or do you feel sidelined as he or she pursues individual plans?

Sharing a purpose together can make the highs and lows more acceptable. Allowing for one another's purpose and supporting each other in times of hardship can mean the difference between fulfilling our purpose early or late in life.

Perhaps a good relationship is having someone close by who will make us do what we can with our lives. This does not mean being an eternally supportive partner. It does involve asking pertinent questions and setting boundaries with each other.

When Heather was being bullied at work, she sought understanding from her partner, Ted. At first Ted sympathised but, when he noticed that Heather was being bullied by friends and acquaintances, too, he became firm. He suggested she stand up for herself. Heather felt abandoned by him. Still, Ted clung to his belief that until she stood up to those who bullied her, she'd attract bullies everywhere she went.

Heather recognised that what Ted was saying was, in fact, correct, and she mustered the courage to begin standing up to her work colleagues. By drawing a line, Ted had encouraged her to be more assertive than she was at first willing to be. He had supported her by refusing to condone her position of weakness.

If you ignore your partner while you pursue your purpose, she or he will probably end up not being a part of either your purpose or your journey.

Being with a partner who shares your vision of your future is joyful, yet this is rare. More common, however, is being with a partner who is prepared to support you in the pursuit of your purpose whether they share your vision or not, because they believe in you and are happy to see you fulfilled.

An example of this occurred with Heath, who supported Stella in her pursuit of a meaningful career. When Stella told Heath that she wanted to move interstate to attend a 24-month course in natural therapies, Heath was shocked. After discussing the possibilities, Heath agreed to contribute more financially to the home over the coming year so that Stella might save the necessary course fees.

Heath had a fulfilling career and did not want to move interstate, so Stella went on without him. They visited one another regularly throughout the 24 months they were apart, and when Stella returned she was able to set up a practice which is currently thriving. Despite the fact that Heath is a plumber and is not interested in natural therapies, he supported Stella because he recognised that she was deriving fulfilment from these areas. Stella remembers this and states that if his time comes to pursue a new career direction, she'll be there to support him in the same way he supported her.

Rewarding relationships can also occur with friends, family members, neighbours or members of a club. Being open to rewarding friendships and relationships on many levels increases the likelihood or your being supported when you most need support in life.

CHAPTER TWELVE

Others' Plans for You

It's natural for parents to have plans for their children as they grow up, and these hopes can sometimes be difficult to shake when the child decides to pursue another path in life. Often this path is different from the lives of those who have gone before them, making it challenging for the parents to support the choice.

For each of us to find our own purpose, we have to be free to decide for ourselves what we want, and what we feel is important to us. However, sometimes parents feel they must push a child in a particular direction.

'Gerard is going to be a lawyer, just like his dad, aren't you, Gerard,' said one mother recently. The boy at her side was six years of age. It is likely that guns, spaceships and cars were more important to him than a career in law.

Sometimes young children do have a fixed idea of what they want to do with their lives. It can be a blessing to have purpose at a young age. More often, however, the discovery of purpose is a process that takes many years. It is important for parents not to rob their children of that choice. Unfortunately, there are some parents who force a son or daughter into a career or life path that makes sound financial sense, but stifles the young person's ability to explore life for themselves.

The process of breaking free of the plans others have for you is an important step towards finding your purpose. The teenage years are perfect for this. There is often strong peer pressure to discard parental values. Coupled with the hormonal changes and the rebellious energy of many teenagers, these years present an opportunity to establish an independent identity, and to toss out parental plans in the process. Many people have to go through their twenties and beyond before they can completely disengage themselves from what their parents want for them, and from the need to win their approval.

There are probably too many men and women in their forties and fifties who were pushed down a path that promised a solid career. They are now experiencing an ongoing mild depression at not being fulfilled by life. There comes a time when it is difficult to begin a new career. Some people find that they are being paid too well to make the change, and it's time to settle in for the long haul.

Often the motivation for parents to push their children into a stable, well-paid career is to ensure security and a stable life. In pursuing this course of action, they risk stifling their children's natural sense of exploration. How can you expect to discover your purpose if you are afraid to explore life?

Sometimes challenging the accepted practice is the first step towards finding what actually suits you. This was evident recently when Marie visited Simon with her nine-year-old son Damian. Simon is a statistician who works from a home office and contracts to large organisations.

'Where do you work?' the boy asked Simon. The man led him from the living room into his home office. Damian stared around the room for a moment before asking, 'But this isn't really where you work, is it?'

'Yes, it is.'

'But it's not a real office.'

'Why not?'

'It's not in the city.'

'No, it's not, and isn't that great? I don't have to spend 45 minutes sitting in traffic every morning and night. I don't have to wear a suit every day and I don't have to listen to everyone else's phone ringing all afternoon. I simply get up in the morning, have breakfast, play a CD and then start work.'

Damian's incredulous look indicated to Simon that the boy thought he was making the whole thing up, so Simon continued, 'I can come home for lunch every day and, if I leave work and find that I've left an important document on my desk, it takes me 10 seconds to collect it. I can play music as I work if I want to. The best part is the lunches.'

'The lunches?'

'Yes. If I'm busy I take only fifteen minutes for lunch but, if I'm up to date with my work, I can have the afternoon off for lunch.'

'Cool,' Damian said, brightening to the possibilities.

'And on my report-writing days, I sometimes don't take a shower or shave all day, and I can sit around in a pair of shorts and a T-shirt as I write. Oh, and I always take Thursdays and Fridays off.' Damian nodded, interested and awakened to new possibilities.

The next generation can benefit from the well-meaning plans made by their parents for them, or they can be greatly hindered. Having to cast off the life others have mapped out for you, and guided you towards, can take a great deal of energy — indeed, years of your life. Then, to discover your own purpose and to pursue it can consume more time.

In my work I've consulted with people who have found the courage to pursue another purpose only after they have retired from their career. It's not too late to begin when you're in your sixties, but the earlier you begin the better.

How do you know if the life you are pursuing is of your own making, or if you're following the directives of others? Try answering the following questions:

- Over the past three years, have you been fulfilled more than 50 per cent of the time?

- Is your life currently the way you imagined it would be five years ago?

- Was the approval of your parents or others a deciding factor in your choice of a career?

- Is the approval of others a deciding factor in your choice of where to live?

- Are others' opinions of you more important than your opinion of yourself?

- Do you feel free to make the important decisions in your life — decisions about your work, home or lifestyle?

ANSWERS: If you answered yes to three or more of the above questions, you need to check your own needs against your desire to please others.

If Jeremy had fulfilled the expectations others had for him as a child, he'd be an electrician now. He'd probably be a poor electrician at that. Jeremy's parents wanted him to have a trade, something to fall back on in case of difficulties. Instead he has become a contented interior designer.

It's a noble hope to want your children to do well, and to encourage them towards careers that ensure a stable living. It's an effort that works particularly well with young men and women who have no idea what they want to do with their working lives.

For those who do have a sense of purpose, however, or just an idea of what they don't want to do, this concept can be destructive. In Jeremy's case, he knew that he didn't want to be an electrician. It's a perfectly fine occupation, but he is unsuited to it.

CHAPTER THIRTEEN

Resisting Others' Expectations

Being unable to resist parental pressure was typified by Lucy, whose parents emigrated from Europe and found embarking on a new life in Australia a formidable challenge. Lucy's father is an accountant. He wanted to see his daughter get into a solid, financially stable career, so he forcefully 'encouraged' Lucy to study pharmacy at university, which she did.

During her final year, Lucy consulted me in despair. She found her grades slipping as a direct result of her loss of interest in the subject.

'I don't want to be a pharmacist,' she explained. 'Standing around all day mixing up drugs in the back of a shop is going to drive me crazy.'

'What would you prefer to do instead?' I asked her.

'I don't know.'

'Is it possible for you to put your head down and successfully complete this course, before deciding what you want to do afterwards?' I probed.

It seemed a waste not to complete the course when she had only four months to go until final exams.

Ordinarily, it's unwise to pursue a career you don't enjoy but, in Lucy's case, as a graduate she'd be free to pursue other studies in almost any chosen direction. She might receive a reward for realising her goal (or her father's goal) of becoming a pharmacist.

'What reward can you give yourself when you finish this course four months from now?' I asked her.

'It's not that simple. After graduation, I have to complete one year of supervised practice with a registered pharmacist. Without this, I cannot practise as a pharmacist.'

'Do you want to practise as a pharmacist?'

'I don't know. If I wanted to do further studies, it would help, because I could work two days a week and earn good money.'

'Okay, so now we are looking at one year and four months. There is a break between the end of the course and the job, I guess.'

'Not really. My father has arranged for me to work with a pharmacist friend of his. The job starts one week after university concludes.'

Upon closer scrutiny, this was a complicated puzzle indeed. Lucy was trapped by her father's determination that she should have a stable career.

'If you are to complete your course and then complete the extra year, what reward can you give yourself after that? If you are going to work hard, you'll want a suitable reward.'

'I'd love to travel overseas, to Europe. I'd like to get away from my family, to live in London or Rome for a year. Ever since I've been in school, my father seems to have been telling me what to do. I want to be free of all that.'

'Okay. So can you save enough while working next year to fly to Europe?'

'I guess so. I'm living at home with my parents, so I don't have many expenses.'

Lucy has since completed the course, concluded her twelve-month trial and is about to set off for Europe. At this point she is contemplating studying again after a six-month holiday. She is examining options that include business management, political science and event management. Her father offered to use his overseas contacts to secure her a job, but Lucy told him she preferred to wait and see what London offered.

Ultimately, it is an excuse to suggest that, as an adult, you cannot upset those whose approval you crave by choosing for yourself. When faced with the choice of pleasing others or yourself, the decision is yours. Although others may initially be upset or disappointed by that decision, things are not always as bad as they first appear. If the hope is simply for you to succeed, when you do, everyone wins — even if the success is in your chosen field, not in the one that had been picked for you.

Approval is important for most of us, but to live our life in a particular way merely for that approval is not healthy. Needing basic recognition socialises us as children and later as adults, and good manners are designed to facilitate smooth social interaction. This benefits everyone we meet. It is quite different from changing our views, our decisions and our life direction for the sake of approval.

For those who continuously feel manipulated by others, asking yourself the questions below on a regular basis may benefit you:

- What do I want?

- Am I happy to do this?

- Is it in my long-term best interests to do this?

- Am I being coerced into this commitment or action?

Coercion was clear in the case of Clarice, whose husband Chet flew into a rage if she didn't fulfil the role he had made for her. When she didn't want to move house for the thirteenth time in fifteen years, he threw vases, shouted at her for hours and threatened her with divorce. By the time she revealed her situation, she was an emotional wreck. The suggestion that she consult a lawyer, in order to see where she stood if she chose to divorce him, was dismissed.

'I don't need a lawyer,' she replied.

'Let me ask you a few questions to see if you do, in fact, need a lawyer. Have Chet's rage attacks grown worse over the years?'

'Yes, they have. He never used to break things, but lately I've had to pack away my good items. Almost everything in the house has been glued together after his attacks.'

Approval is important for most of us, but to live our life in a particular way merely for that approval is not healthy.

'Is he flying into a temper tantrum over inconsequential things these days?'

'Yes.'

'Has he threatened you with physical violence?'

'Yes.'

'Do you think he'd threaten you with physical violence if you were a man of his size and build?' '

'I guess not.'

'Of course not. A man the same size would be likely to punch him hard on the nose if he tried that sort of standover tactic with him. This makes your husband a bully. Bullies intimidate people who are smaller and pose little threat to them. Now, one more question. Has he hit you in the past?'

'Only once, but he was very apologetic afterwards. He bought me flowers and took me out to dinner.'

'So, if I was to ask you for a date, suggesting an expensive restaurant and holding out a bunch of flowers, but also mentioning that I'd have to hit you beforehand to make the date complete for me, do you think you'd want to go out with me?'

'No. I don't like violence.'

'So why do you accept it from Chet?'

'Well, it's not that simple. He's under a lot of pressure at work, which is only getting worse. They are cutting back staff numbers, and he has more work than ever before.'

'So, let's see if I've got this right. Pretend that I'm Chet, and I'm overloaded with responsibilities, deadlines and pressure. I'm exhausted when I arrive home from work each night. Am I on track so far?'

'Yes.'

'I collapse when I arrive home — later than I used to because I have more work than ever. I sit in front on the TV staring at nothing before I fall asleep. Is this close to the picture?'

'Yes.'

'I'm so tired, so completely exhausted that all I have the energy to do is eat dinner and fall asleep.'

'Yes.'

'Then how do you account for the fact that I have the energy to fly into a rage when I need to? How do I find the energy to hit you and to terrorise you from time to time? That sort of behaviour requires a great deal of energy, don't you think?'

'Yes, but it doesn't happen all the time.'

'That's true, but I guess you tiptoe around in case tonight's the night ...'

'Yes, you're right.'

'And by your own admission, it is happening more frequently than it used to.'

'Yes,' she mumbled.

'Is it fair to say that you feel the tension rising within your body in the late afternoon, long before Chet arrives home?'

'Yes.'

'Are you a prisoner in your own life, in your own home?'

'Sometimes.'

'Do you need a lawyer?'

'Chet just needs help. He's stressed and overworked.'

'That's Chet's choice. You also need help, and you're the one who has sought it. Chet isn't here crying because he has bullied his wife and children. He's not seeking ways to manage his anger. Ted is only visible in the fear he has instilled within you. He has left his fingerprints on your heart. Your bruises are internal, yet still you make excuses for him.'

'He just needs some help, some understanding.'

'Yes, he does. Are you the one to give him this, or do you think it might be better if it came from a counsellor or a psychologist?'

'I've tried to understand him, but it's not working.'

'It is possible that, if you allow this situation to develop for another five or ten years, Chet will turn into a killer, and your name will be immortalised on a piece of marble. Is that what you want? When your children press up against you, do you want them to feel the warmth of your flesh or the smooth cool marble of a tombstone?'

Clarice consulted a family lawyer, who briefly outlined her choices. It was an important process to have a trained professional inform her of her legal options. The lawyer also detailed her husband's legal obligations should she decide to leave him and start a new life for herself. It's one thing to dream about getting out of a situation, but it's altogether different when you sit down with a professional adviser to learn exactly what your options are.

CHAPTER FOURTEEN

Retrieving Control of Your Life

If you find yourself living a life others have planned for you, while your own plans languish in the far reaches of your mind, the *Retrieving Control of Your Life* exercise on page 78 is for you.

Firstly, you need to take note of how others expect you to live or behave. A good example of expectations occurred with Nathan.

Nathan was sharing a rented house with a young woman. Soon it became apparent that her expectations of him were stifling him. When Maxine moved in, she seemed to be an independent and assertive woman. Over the months, Nathan found himself listening to her complain about her problems. He felt useful listening to her when she needed someone.

Shortly after her arrival, Maxine cancelled her regular weekly session with her therapist because she was being heard at home. When she separated from her partner, Nathan was there to listen. When she experienced problems with her boss or her co-workers, he was the one to help her to make sense of things.

Then Nathan received a promotion and was less available for Maxine. She'd arrive home from work to find him in the spare room, working at his notebook computer, often until late in the evening. He often heard her pacing about the house. He sensed that she was waiting for him to stop working so that she was able to 'download her day' and together they might make sense of it.

Nathan realised that he didn't want the role of counsellor when they were in fact co-tenants. He admitted that continually lending Maxine an ear night after night was draining, especially when he had a looming deadline for a work project.

Gently he retreated from her, making himself less available as he pursued his work. In response Maxine became more determined to attract his attention. At first she ventured into the spare room to ask Nathan how his day had been. He replied something like, 'It's still unfolding', while staring at the computer screen before him. He realised that her question was simply an opener so that he'd respond with the same question, and thus allow her to get the events of her day off her chest.

Maxine's behaviour is a natural one for partners who share a house together, or for co-tenants who have plenty of time to chat, but since Nathan's work continued into the evenings, she was, in fact, interrupting him. He recalled the few times he had phoned her at work with a question, only to be given brief answers and the distinct impression that he was interrupting her busy schedule.

Throughout the next month, Maxine attempted to attract Nathan's attention by various means, including flirting with him. This was despite the fact that both of them had partners, and she wasn't really interested in Nathan.

In frustration one day he diplomatically suggested that she return to her therapy sessions or find a more attentive partner. He said he wasn't qualified to advise her on her life and no longer had time to listen to her, because work deadlines demanded his attention.

The art of slipping free of the chains in which others have held you can be tricky, as those around you may be resentful when you don't live up to their expectations. I'm not talking of the disappointment that comes from broken promises or emotional neglect, but rather of the resentment that can accompany disillusionment.

If others fall in love with you with the expectation that you will make them happy, how do you think they'll feel if you turn around and tell them that you're not responsible for their happiness? They may experience anger, desperation or deep grief. They may also feel alone in the world and depressed that their hopes have been dashed on the rocks of reality.

You may well expect a backlash when you tell them how you intend changing your life or your living patterns. They may feel that their disillusionment is justified, as is your yearning for independence. If you have been fulfilling their needs or fuelling their hopes that you can make them happy, don't expect them to support you in your quest to be free or your pursuit of your own goals in life. The very fact that you have a clear sense of purpose may be enough to upset others.

If you have been held back in your quest for purpose by those who have a great deal emotionally invested in keeping you where you are in life, breaking free is a delicate process. When you most need support to spread your wings and to take flight, those around you feel threatened. They may consciously or unconsciously attempt to clip your wings in order to keep you 'in your place'. If you ask them for support and rely on them to help you, it may take many attempts before you can fly away towards your true purpose.

This is one of the reasons a counsellor or independent coach is recommended. Support from someone who is independent and who has less invested in keeping you where you are can make your first flight much more relaxing, requiring less effort.

Forget about trying to reason with those who have the most to lose if you pursue your purpose or a goal that conflicts with what they have in mind for you. In the case of Maxine and Nathan, Maxine rarely felt listened to sufficiently. This was because the two people she most wanted to hear her, didn't. Her parents were too busy to notice her as she grew up. So now she experiences a deep, searing need to be heard, which is rarely satisfied.

If you are prepared to be responsible for your own path in life, you have to be prepared to allow others the same opportunity. In the case of Maxine, Nathan realised that by concentrating on his work in the evenings, he was causing her pain. He also realised, however, that if he spent his evenings listening to her and ignoring his work deadlines, he might lose his promotion. Maxine wasn't prepared to write Nathan's reports for him, and he now wasn't prepared to ignore his needs in favour of hers. He felt sensitive to her pain, but recognised that, in time, she'd become more independent or find someone else to listen to her.

Maxine did find another friend prepared to listen to her, while Nathan observed from a distance. Her new friend, Lucia, was in love with her. Nathan watched as Maxine starved Lucia of the love she sought. He could see Lucia hoping that Maxine might fulfil her need for love, while Maxine hoped that Lucia might satisfy the hunger she had to be heard by another person. Both of them starved emotionally until Nathan again suggested to Maxine that she return to her therapist. Gradually, her resentment of Nathan dissipated as her therapist helped her.

The exercise on the next page may need to be completed for each person in your life who you feel has plans for you, or has something invested in your remaining on your current path. It may help you to differentiate between those who want you to be happy and those who want you to make them happy. Burn your responses afterwards if you feel the need for complete privacy.

Not all friendships or relationships are equal, beneficial or likely to feed you emotionally, mentally or spiritually. The following exercise is designed to help you to reassess your friendships and relationships, to determine whether or not they prevent you from pursuing your purpose. Often it is not a case of someone bending your will to theirs, or overtly manipulating you towards compliance with their plans for you. It can be as simple as recognising that your need for approval is keeping you prisoner.

RETRIEVING CONTROL OF YOUR LIFE EXERCISE

Select one friend, family member or your partner.

- Are you able to be yourself while with this person?

- Are you able to reveal yourself to this person without feeling judged?

- Does this person ever reveal him/herself to you?

- When this person has revealed him/herself to you in the past, have you been judgmental?

- Do you feel safe enough to share your dreams and hopes with this person?

- Do you regularly feel burdened by this person's needs?

- Do you regularly feel obligated to fulfil this person's needs?

- Do you want this person to be happy?

- Do you have expectations about an appropriate life for this person?

- Do you sense that he/she wants you to be happy?

- Do you sense he/she has expectations about an appropriate life for you?

- On balance, who has the strongest needs when you are together?

Many years ago Sean received a clairvoyant reading from a woman who asked him the following questions:

'Have you proved yourself yet? It seems to me that you have gone along with others' expectations of you, hoping to win their approval, but they weren't even looking. Have you proved to them and to yourself that you can be conservative and good? If so, isn't it time you started doing what you really want to do?'

Sean was shocked. The clairvoyant had appraised his life succinctly. His stomach churned, and he felt physically sick. The thought of living the life he was living for another ten years really sickened him.

It's not that Sean's life was tragic or wayward. It simply wasn't right for him. Working as a clerk in an office was driving him crazy. He'd arrive at 8:45 am and complete his workload by 1:00 pm. He'd spend the rest of the day writing poetry and dreaming of doing something else — anything else — for a living.

After he received that clairvoyant reading, it occurred to Sean that when he is eventually buried, it won't matter at all to him what those surviving say about him. If he's buried amidst scandalous circumstances and he dies doing what he loves to do, then he'll be happy. What benefit will there be for him to die of sheer boredom, his only reward being that those surviving think well of him?

In the 1980s two close friends and Sean planned to travel through Europe on the 'grand tour'. He was hopeless with saving and when the time came to buy the tickets, he wasn't ready. Jenny and Joanne left without him. He still has the postcards they sent while away.

They had a fabulous time for almost eight months. Sean missed them while they were away. Not long after they returned, Jenny died, so an adventure they might have shared cannot be repeated this lifetime. How many similar adventures have you also missed or postponed?

CHAPTER FIFTEEN

Power and Responsibility

Are you ready for the responsibility that accompanies power? If you fail miserably to reach your goals or feel you have failed in life generally and you blame others for your plight, you absolve yourself of responsibility. Take your parents, for example. You can wax lyrical about how well you might have done if only they had been different. If only they had been more encouraging, less structured, stricter with you, richer, taller, more inclined to travel the world, or even if they'd just been more open to living closer to the equator, your life might be different now.

If you decide to step away from the plans others have for you, you are faced with complete responsibility for your life. Being honest with yourself and others means saying, 'I am responsible for my success or my failure to realise my goals in life'.

How do you think you might feel if someone asked you what you had done with your life and you answered in the following way?

'I began with lots of dreams and went nowhere really. I wasted ten years in a job I hated and then ran up a huge debt while I waited for success as an artist — which never came. Realising that I was a painter of only moderate talent, I gave it away to move out here to run this kiosk by the beach. The money is terrible, but at least I have a view of the sea and I can paint.'

Now is the time to be honest with yourself. If you don't like the idea of not having anyone to blame or to hide behind when things fall over and plans are abandoned, seriously consider the benefits of giving responsibility for your life to others.

When someone else controls you, there are benefits. Some of these are listed below:

- You don't have to think for yourself.

- You're not responsible when things go wrong. Others may blame you, but you can always argue that you were doing what you were taught/told to do.

- You are free to dream about the life you might live if you were free to choose for yourself, without having to make any real efforts to test your dreams in the real world.

- Those whose plans you are fulfilling may take care of you (as long as you fulfil your role).

- Once you have perfected your role in life, you can cruise through the years without too many surprises.

- The bottom line is that you know the price you have to pay in order to be loved. It may be a heavy toll or a small fee, but it is an agreed price (unconsciously) and, in paying it, you receive the love you have earned.

If the above list appeals to you, be honest about it. If, on the other hand, you are prepared to take responsibility for your own life, meeting your own needs and determining your own direction, this choice, too, comes with a price tag, one that is less predictable.

The price you may have to pay when you decide to take your life into your hands may involve:

- Exclusion from your family, circle of friends or club.

- Hearing negative opinions of yourself from those around you.

- Being deprived of financial support from those who have a great deal to lose by your lifestyle changes.

- Failing publicly in your goals, which may become exciting gossip for those you leave behind.

- Succeeding beyond your wildest dreams, and having to learn how to cope with your new-found wealth, social circle, fame and the accompanying opportunities.

- Being responsible when things go wrong; putting up with taunts from former friends or family: 'I told you so', or with their gloating over your failures.

- Having to think for yourself when important decisions are required. (This doesn't mean that you can't consult experienced professionals to help with your decisions.)

- Taking care of yourself when things go wrong.

- Being lonely when you reach the pinnacle of your chosen field.

- Feeling unloved.

This last point, that you may not be loved, is probably the strongest reason for not taking charge of one's own life. The fear of being alone and unloved in the world makes many people so terrified that they become voluntary life prisoners. Try the following questionnaire:

DO YOU FEAR BEING UNLOVED?

- What happens when the person who loves you finds someone else to love?

- What happens if you are physically unable to perform your role?

- What happens when you discover that the love you are receiving is not love at all, but simply a reward for performance?

- What happens when all your efforts and performance for love fail to generate the appropriate response in your partner or loved ones?

- What becomes of your wild wolf, whose spirit hungers for freedom and a taste of the other life, where consequences are determined by your decisions and choices?

- What happens if you look into the mirror one day and decide that you don't like what you have become?

- What becomes of your passion?

- What happens when you tire of being good?

- Is being loved by a particular person enough to stave off thoughts of who else might be out there for you if you were to search?

After considering the price that you may have to pay and the obstacles you might face in taking charge of your own life, let's examine what you may gain by taking these steps.

At the dawn of each day, you might plan your goals for the day. If you do, then you're likely to review those goals at the close of the day.

At the beginning of each year, you can make a list of goals or resolutions for the year ahead. Regularly reviewing your goals reduces the likelihood of overlooking any single goal.

It is important to make lists that are both achievable and realistic. A friend of mine gave up making them each year because, she said, she was disillusioned at never seeing one goal realised. When asked what she usually listed, she replied, 'Things like world peace and personal enlightenment'. Perhaps she might opt for the other extreme: giving up cigarettes, bobsledding, night skydiving, eating meat and drinking whisky. Considering she is a non-smoking, non-drinking vegetarian who has never been skydiving and doesn't know what a bobsled is, she'll be able to fulfil all of her list and proudly state that 'all it takes is willpower'.

If she listed her goals like that for a few years running, she'd be booked on a speakers' circuit, to tell the rest of us how easy it is to keep resolutions. Setting realistic goals is rewarding and a motivation for taking on bigger goals next time. First you crawl, then you walk, then you run and, finally, you dance.

Setting goals starts with the day and then progresses to the week. When you have mastered weekly goals, you set monthly ones. When you are familiar with what you can achieve in a month, you move on to yearly aims. Then you can tackle ten-year goals and, finally, life goals.

One of the rewards of taking responsibility for your life is that you can go after what really matters to you. Others might tell you that you are lucky and that things come easy for you because . . . In reality, the less people actually follow their dreams, the more room there is for you to do so.

When you step out of the accepted routine, all sorts of possibilities open up to you. Taking one or two days off during the working week instead of at weekends can illustrate this fact. You can choose to spend an afternoon snorkelling on near-empty beaches. If you want to go shopping or see a film at the cinema, there are none of the queues so characteristic of the weekends.

The typical working man or woman has a restricted existence in some countries. During the school holidays, the cost of a room in a hotel or a beachside holiday apartment goes up because of increased demand. The police usually double the penalties for driving offences during peak holiday periods, and those taking holidays at that time often have to queue for everything they want.

A friend of mine spends over $65 per week in bridge and freeway tolls driving to and from work. That's $3120 per year if he takes four weeks off each year. That's four weeks off to stand in queues and pay top dollar for his hotel room.

Taking charge of one's life is something that everyone can do. Of course, some things are inevitable. You'll still pay tax, grow older and eventually die, but it's what you do in the intervening years that makes your old age and death rewarding or a relief to get away from a life filled with obligations.

Fear paralyses some of us, and we'll deal with that in the next chapter. List below the things you want from the next twelve months. Be realistic and be honest.

MY GOALS FOR THE NEXT 12 MONTHS:

CHAPTER SIXTEEN

Tackling Fear

Fear is a natural and, indeed, a healthy part of life. If you experience no fear whatsoever, it is unlikely that you will survive for very long. Rational fears are linked to survival, our most basic need. It is important to understand that you are not being asked in this chapter to ignore genuine fears about real issues.

Real issues include such things as your telephone bill, having a suitable place to live and maintaining your physical health. Deny these things for too long and you'll soon find life very uncomfortable. An example of this type of denial occurred with a friend named Tania, who was flat out in bed with influenza when I visited her. I made us both a cup of tea and returned to find her repeating an affirmation aloud. 'What are you saying?' I asked.

'Oh, I'm just reminding myself that I am healthy and I'm fine, and that I'm getting better all the time.' At this point she stepped out of bed towards the bedside chair and promptly fell flat on her face. She had become dizzy through exhaustion due to her condition.

'That's one powerful affirmation you have there,' I stated calmly as I helped her back into bed.

To demonstrate this point, if you have no fear of poverty and are convinced that when you leave your job, the universe will support you, then leave it and wait for the universe — unless you have passive income from investments, a lack of fear is unlikely to support you financially.

We will examine ways to deal with fears that feel life-threatening, but are actually about situations that can be solved.

It has long been understood that the way to tackle fear is to face it. This is easier said than done. How you deal with the problems you face is often initially determined by your upbringing. Children observe their parents or teachers dealing with problems on a daily basis. They often observe more than the problems. They also notice the approach those adults use to solve their problems.

An example of this occurred with Martin who, as a child, used to see his mother writing cheques late at night once a month to pay the bills. When the other children were asleep, she cleaned the kitchen, with Martin's help, and then sat down with the outstanding accounts spread out across the table. After determining which were the most important ones to pay, she wrote the cheques and put them in their envelopes for posting the following day. Not once did it occur to Martin to ask why he never saw his father write a cheque or pay a bill. As a child, he assumed that it was something women did.

As an adult, Martin repeats his mother's pattern. He clears the table in his home office and spreads the outstanding accounts across it before writing cheques and addressing the envelopes for them. It is an approach that has served him well, and he seems pleased that his mother taught it to him so thoroughly.

He learned quite a different pattern from his father. When an account arrived, Martin's father often panicked and proclaimed his inability to pay it at all, with statements like, 'We'll never be able to pay this on time. They'll come chasing us, for sure. How on earth are we supposed to pay this?' At this point his mother usually snatched the account from his grasp before he could work himself into a lather. She put it with the other accounts and reviewed it when payment time came.

The adult Martin sometimes found himself following his father's pattern: 'Oh my God! This is outrageous! How do they expect me to pay this?' He'd stew over the account for a few hours or even a few days before finally placing it in the 'in-tray', to be reviewed and paid at the next cheque-writing session.

One day he found himself staring at a $12,000 account that he had to pay in four months. He worked himself into a state of semi-hysteria. Needless to say, his melodramatic ranting did not assist with the payment. When he consulted me, we devised a method together to address what at first appeared to be insurmountable problems. It is called the *Three Case Scenarios*. It is not designed to solve your problems, but to help you to gain a better perspective and to examine your hopes and fears. Those who complete this exercise usually find themselves at peace with the steps they are preparing to take.

THE THREE CASE SCENARIOS

- **THE WORST CASE SCENARIO**
  Write down the worst possible outcome(s) to your present dilemma. Be creative and imaginative with your depiction of the outcome.

- **THE AVERAGE CASE SCENARIO**
  Name the likely outcome(s) to your present situation. You can base your answer on previous outcomes for you or friends who have experienced a similar dilemma.

- **THE BEST POSSIBLE CASE SCENARIO**
  Describe the best possible outcome(s) to your present situation. Be creative. Look for opportunities that might stem from problems.

The purpose of listing possible outcomes is to put your fears and hopes down on paper. This can help you to acknowledge what you really fear and hope for. It may also allow you to determine from reading your lists how you are approaching your problem. In most cases it will be resolved according to the average case scenario, but it doesn't hurt to know what the possibilities are if the situation takes a turn for the worse or for the better.

Beside each possible outcome on your worst case scenario, write a solution. This helps to address your deepest fears and gives you some concrete possibilities if you actually have to face them.

Beside each possible issue on your average case scenario list, place a possible solution. This helps to address the issues arising from an average resolution to your problem.

For each outcome on your best possible case scenario, set down a possible solution or action to accompany it. These actions are more likely to be celebrations, if they eventuate.

Tom illustrates this technique in action. He was told by his mechanic that his car was about to expire or explode, as it was old and plagued with problems. Tom couldn't afford another car, but he was also unable to continue repairing his old car as it was costing a small fortune. In a state of panic, he consulted me to help him review his options. We commenced with the worst case scenario and it went something like this:

- TOM'S WORST CASE SCENARIO
  The car collapses and Tom is stranded in peak-hour-traffic. He is unable to afford the repairs. The fuel line springs a leak again, and it explodes into flames as he is driving to work one morning.

  Tom buys a new car and then loses his job.

  Tom's new car is repossessed by the finance company when he cannot keep up the payments. He now has a bad credit rating.

  Tom's new car is stolen one week after he takes delivery and, to reduce costs, it was not insured for theft.

  Tom's present car breaks down, and he is left walking everywhere.

- TOM'S AVERAGE CASE SCENARIO

   Tom uses his old car as a trade-in on a cheap new car.

   If he loses his job, he sells the new car.

   Tom purchases a late-model used car that will suffice for a few years.

   Tom moves closer to the office or he uses public transport to ensure a stress-free journey to and from work each day. He saves for twelve months to buy another car.

   Tom secures a new job that includes a car as part of the salary package.

- TOM'S BEST POSSIBLE CASE SCENARIO:

   Tom asks for a salary increase to help with the purchase of a new car. (This also confirms the stability of his employment.)

   Tom buys a new car and insures it so that he can use it for three or four years without worrying.

   Tom works hard to increase his salary again in the next three years or to secure a better-paid job, one that allows him to purchase another car in three years' time.

   Tom enters every lottery available for two weeks, in the hope of winning a new car or the money to purchase one.

   Tom scours the deceased estate sales in his local newspaper in search of a late-model car that is being sold cheaply.

Now Tom adds a list of possible solutions to take in each eventuality. He begins with the worst case scenario.

- THE WORST CASE SCENARIO SOLUTIONS LIST:

   If the car breaks down, it can be left where it is or towed cheaply by the automobile association to his local mechanic.

   He can purchase a fire extinguisher for the car.

   If he loses his job, he can use the new car to enable him to find a new job. A reliable car gives him access to a wider area in which to search for jobs. He can also leave the car aside until he can afford to run it again, or he can simply sell it.

A new car can be used to transport him to job interviews.

Tom can pay to have an engine immobiliser and an alarm installed, to reduce the likelihood of the car being stolen.

If his current car breaks down, Tom can keep fit by walking.

Tom's average case scenario does not require solutions. The solutions are already shown in the alternatives. Should his situation be resolved via any of the best possible case scenario options, he plans to celebrate with a long lunch and a bottle of champagne.

In reviewing these lists, Tom is highlighting the possibilities and listing how he plans to deal with each eventuality if it arises. Naturally, it is possible that he will face a problem or an opportunity that he hadn't anticipated. If this occurs, he can return to his lists, put it where it belongs and add a solution, if one is required.

Where most of us go wrong is that we form only one of these lists in our mind and plan for only one possible eventuality. Some get bogged down in the worst case scenario, planning their funeral 20 years ahead of the fact. Others expect only calm seas and then tremble when they are facing down a storm. By taking time to examine the worst to the best possibilities, you can be better prepared. If lightning strikes you and it wasn't listed in your worst case scenario, you won't need the list anyway.

Now you have an opportunity to list your worst, average and best case scenarios in relation to one major issue in your life. Take three pieces of paper, one for each scenario.

- Outline the issue. Keep it simple; for example, your current work situation or relationship.

- List the worst possible eventuality in point form. Leave room for possible solutions for each point.

- List the average scenario in the same simple point form. Leave room for possible solutions here, too.

- List the best possible scenario. Again, leave room for possible solutions for each point.

- Now list those practical solutions for each point on each list.

- Review your lists and review your issue in the light of your lists.

- You are now ready to tackle your issue. Feel free to add to your lists as you go.

Fear will control you whether you acknowledge it or not.

If you want to be dramatic about your issues, then go ahead and give it your best shot. Remember, however, that drama belongs on the stage and, unless you're being paid to dramatise your life, it's probably better to save your energy for more rewarding pursuits.

In simple terms it pays to recognise fear, for fear can control you whether you acknowledge it or not. If you acknowledge fear, you have a chance to determine if your fears are well founded, based on past experiences or simply a habit you have formed to prevent change.

It is important to recognise your preferred approach to problems, to see if the planned approach is the best strategy for the present situation. If it doesn't appear to be the most appropriate strategy for the current circumstances, it is time to examine new and more relevant strategies. As you incorporate more strategies into your life, you increase your ability to deal with a wider range of issues or challenges as they present themselves.

CHAPTER SEVENTEEN

Daring to Hope

To some of us, hope is a slender candle burning unprotected in a fierce wind. These people expect it to be extinguished. For others, hope is as natural as breathing. They truly understand the concept that 'it is better to light one candle than to curse the darkness'. These people, in their darkest hour, when grief and despair sit beside them, light one candle to rekindle hope.

For some, hope alone is enough to carry us forward until life offers us better opportunities, while for others, all hoping is hopeless unless they are actively doing something practical and constructive towards their goals. Some people maintain hope in the face of all that life brings, while still others see their hopes crushed — extinguished as the beauty of a flower torn to pieces by the unrelenting elements.

One of the most powerful ways to nurture hope is to acknowledge it. The Acknowledging Hope exercise on page 99 is designed to help you name those things for which you hope and examine ways to nurture those hopes and dreams. The final phase involves taking real steps towards them.

Genuine hope sometimes stems from our cells and our bones. This hope can be illusive, as in the case of Anita.

Anita lost her first child, Toni, to meningitis when she was only three years old. For months afterwards, Anita seemed to be drowning in a sea of overwhelming grief. Friends rallied around her at first but, as the weeks passed, they slipped back into their busy lives, leaving Anita with a gaping hole in her life.

Each morning she climbed out of bed, stumbling through the day ahead, carrying the hope that one day she might have a reason to get up in the morning. She had reached the place where pain has no words. In her mute state, she silently screamed for her lost daughter, but no-one heard her screams.

As Anita reached new depths of despair, she discovered hope's twin. Hope and despair are never too far away from one another, yet each demands that you sit with him exclusively.

Eight months after Toni's death, Anita's marriage collapsed. Her husband left her. She faced more turmoil, losing interest in herself, her life and her friends, just spending evenings at home with her memories. She had two large photographs of Toni made into jigsaw puzzles and spent hours piecing them together as she wept.

One afternoon her best friend Juliana arrived unexpectedly with a gift. It was another jigsaw puzzle, but this one was based on a photo of Anita and Juliana together in better times. Anita completed the new puzzle repeatedly, and slowly allowed Juliana back into her heart. One day, this good friend arrived with still another jigsaw puzzle, this one based on a photograph of Anita and several of her friends. Both figuratively and physically, Anita was being helped to piece her life back together. Juliana knew there was no way to replace little Toni, but she also realised that she had to rekindle Anita's hope in life as being worth living again.

Hope is sometimes very fragile, whereas false hope is hopeless. Juliana was unable to force Anita's hope to return, as it comes back when it is ready. As it happened, she approached Anita at the right time, to strengthen and rekindle her hope. Now, whenever Anita wants to include something new in her life or to expand her physical or emotional horizons, she takes a photo and has it made into a jigsaw puzzle. She has taken up water-skiing, fencing, ballroom dancing, snorkelling and ice-skating, with a jigsaw puzzle for each pursuit. At last count, she had 74 puzzles, and she can almost piece together the portraits of Toni blindfolded.

To fulfil your purpose, you need to act with conviction. This conviction is based on the hope that it is possible for you to realise your purpose. This hope needs to be acknowledged, rekindled and strengthened. The exercise on the next page is an opportunity to do just that. Be prepared to burn or otherwise destroy your answers for reasons of privacy, if you need to.

What are you presently doing to strengthen your hopes for the items you have listed in the first four points?

For those of us who sit more often with despair than with hope, despair too will eventually tire of our company. When he does, he'll slip away silently, leaving hope to revisit you. One difficulty is that even a minute spent with despair can seem like a long, exhausting week.

Great achievements can spring from great hopes, because these hopes can lead to plans, and plans in turn beget actions. That's the way hopes are realised.

If you perceive the process as a jigsaw puzzle, then your hopes are depicted by the picture on the box. The pieces contained within are your skills and talents. For success, you need to find a way to assemble the tiny pieces into the picture on the cover.

Your hope might be to become wealthy. You clearly picture in your mind the level of wealth you desire and then set about making your goal a reality. The pieces of the jigsaw might represent courses of study you undertake, investments you make, friends who support or assist you, a move to another locality, a marriage, children and health issues. How you assemble the pieces is entirely up to you. Action must accompany hope for tangible results.

ACKNOWLEDGING HOPE EXERCISE

- List three **physical** things you hope for. An example was George, who was ill with cancer and wanted to attend an ice-skating competition in Europe. His poor health threatened to prevent him from attending, even as a spectator. George's physical hope was to be well enough to attend the skating championship.

- List three **emotional** things you hope for. George's emotional hope was that he'd be supported while visiting Europe. He had relatives nearby and hoped they'd look after him emotionally.

- List three **mental** things you hope for. George hoped to measure the talent and precision of the upcoming skaters, having been a champion skater himself in his early years.

- List three **spiritual** things you hope for. George hoped to feel inspired by the graceful precision of the skaters.

- List three things you once held hopes for, but now no longer do. In George's case, he had hoped to repeat his success in the international skating competition seventeen years earlier.

- List three things you dare not hope for, lest your hopes be dashed.

- List three things those around you hope for which trigger feelings of anger or resentment.

CHAPTER EIGHTEEN

Rewards

The fundamental rewards of discovering and pursuing your life's purpose include inner peace, fulfilment, passion translated into action, meaningful victories and pride of a life well lived. The bizarre thing is that when you succeed with those things you love, more often than not, others say things like, 'It's okay for you to do that because you have talent/support/fewer children to support/are taller than me etc'.

When you are attempting to change your behaviour to put your life on track, you can expect resistance from those around you. Once you have your life on track, those who attempted to prevent you from changing often take a different approach. They no longer consciously or unconsciously attempt to sabotage you, but instead offer you a new place in their minds. This is a place specially for those people who are different from the rest. In some cases they will go out of their way to assist you towards your new goals, feeling a sense of pride that they helped you towards an even greater success. The greater your success, the greater the range of opportunities open to you. These opportunities are usually only open to those who have taken care of their basic needs and are free to explore life's possibilities.

Having an awareness that life becomes easier is the first step. Some of us think that more success brings more responsibilities and that life gets harder as you realise your goals. This was illustrated one day many years ago when Geoff, a car parking attendant, was parking a large Mercedes-Benz. He overheard a man say to his partner, 'I've heard that they are hard to drive and very hard to park'. Geoff asked the simple question, 'Why would anyone buy a luxury car if it was hard to drive?' He then mentioned that he parked it using only two fingers as the steering was so light. Motorists who can afford a luxury car aren't interested in struggling; they simply want to comfortably arrive at their desired destinations.

Those who have discovered and pursued their life's purpose know that it is the most rewarding thing you can do. It sounds obvious when it is stated, but people respond well to rewards for efforts — from five-year-old Janine eating her dinner in order to have her dessert, to the CEO of a multinational company receiving a performance bonus of a block of shares in the company. We usually work harder when rewards are meaningful.

Whether pursuing your life purpose or long-term goals, rewards along the way are essential if you are to remain motivated. Very few people can delay gratification for long periods of time, so small rewards along the path to success make the journey more enjoyable. Sometimes people argue that the reward at the end is sufficient, but if so, why do so few people actually realise their goals?

Having broken a long-term goal down into many smaller steps, you then decide which points merit a reward. For clients who have a history of abandoned goals, many small rewards are needed early on in order to establish a pattern of effort bringing results, as well as results bringing rewards. For these clients, two processes are occurring at once: a goal is being pursued, and a new pattern is being established. This positive new pattern will eventually make it easier to pursue larger, longer-term goals. One big mistake many people make is giving inappropriate rewards for efforts. Carmella made this mistake when she decided to write a book. She had an idea for a novel and felt the urge to turn it into a book before life took her in another direction. She began by seeking assistance in outlining the required steps to a successful novel. I asked her some questions to see if writing a novel was something she might do well:

- Do you read many novels?

- Do you like to write?

- Have you written any short stories, feature articles or books before?

- Do you have somewhere quiet to write undisturbed?

- Can you express yourself through the written word?

- How long are you prepared to devote to this project?

- Do you observe those around you in order to notice character traits and speech patterns?

Carmella was taken aback at having her writing treated as a project, but that's what it was. I explained that if she planned to spend months discussing the 'creative process' or 'her intrinsic need to find the voice of a character in her novel', she'd need a great deal more help than was presently being offered. She gave me the impression of someone with a romantic vision of a writer's life. It appeared that she had put more effort into imagining the dinner table conversations than the writing and editing aspect of the project.

She left the session feeling dejected, but it is difficult to support someone who is dreaming about something they are not prepared to do. Potential success is not actual success. Carmella had been reminded that potential doesn't always translate to realistic possibilities. A week later she was back, with a more realistic view of writing her novel, and determined to see the project through to completion. I asked her what completion was for her.

- Will the novel be complete when you have written the final page?

- Or when it has been to an independent editor and you have made all the suggested changes?

- When you have sent it off to a publisher?

- When you have a contract to publish?

- Will you consider it done when you hold your first published copy?

- Will completion of your author's tour to publicise the novel end the process?

- Perhaps it will be complete when you read your first review in a newspaper or a magazine?

- Will it be complete when you have your first copy published in another language?

This series of questions was designed to determine if Carmella wanted to write a novel or to be a writer. Writing a novel is one process, whereas becoming a writer is more involved.

She decided that she wanted to write a novel. Over the next three weeks, she laid out the steps to her goal. Carmella realised that she might add or remove steps as she proceeded, due to circumstances. The steps are flexible, but it is reassuring to have them in mind before commencing.

Carmella hadn't written a novel before. In fact, she had limited experience with writing generally and, as a result, she needed several small rewards early on in the process, to establish a pattern and to keep her motivated towards her longer-term goal. The steps and rewards are listed over the page.

STEPS

- Outline the chapters of the novel.

- Write each chapter title on a post-it note and place these onto a large (A2) sheet of paper. This will serve as a map for the novel. Any additions or deletions of chapters are recorded on this page. As each chapter is written (in any order), tick off the corresponding post-it note.

- Outline each of the characters, including their name, age, interests, hopes, fears and shadow side.

- Decide on a setting; for instance, modern-day Kansas or 19th-century Paris.

- Research the setting.

- Establish regular times each week to write.

- Write the first chapter.

- Review the first chapter.

- Write two more chapters.

- Review the process.

- Complete the novel.

- Have the novel independently edited before it is shown to a publisher.

- Make any required or suggested corrections after editing.

- Write an outline for the publisher to read.

- Write up a short proposal for the publisher.

- Have an independent editor edit the proposal and outline.

- Approach several fiction publishers.

- If a contract is offered, consult a lawyer experienced with book contracts to go over the contract with you.

- Sign the contract.

- Write the back cover text.

- Make any required or suggested corrections with the publisher's editorial team.

- Receive your first copy of your novel.

- Celebrate.

- Cooperate with the publisher to publicise the book through bookstore appearances, etc.

When Carmella saw the completed list of steps, she was overwhelmed by the enormity of it all. On one piece of paper she saw hundreds of hours of work ahead of her. So, to shorten her view, she folded the page in half, obscuring the later steps.

'Focus on steps one and two,' she told herself and set to work. Her major reward for successfully completing and publishing the novel was to be a two-week holiday on a tropical island in Queensland. To maintain the focus on this reward, Carmella cut out a few images of the perfect tropical island and pasted them up where she might see them regularly. She put pictures from a travel brochure on her home computer, where she was doing her writing.

Next she outlined her rewards. Keeping in mind the fact that she had not written a book before, small rewards were placed at the end of each initial step, in order to set a positive pattern. Carmella told me what rewards she wanted, which resulted in the list below.

STEPS WITH REWARDS

- Outline the chapters of the novel.
  REWARD: Buy a novel by a favourite author.

- Write each chapter title on a post-it note and place these onto a large (A2) sheet of paper. This served as a map for the novel. Any additions or deletions of chapters are recorded on this page.
  REWARD: Dinner at her favourite Thai restaurant with a friend.

- Outline each of the characters.
  REWARD: Attend a talk by a local author.

- Decide on a setting.
- Research the setting.
- Establish regular times each week to write.
- Write the first chapter.
  REWARD: Pick and price the holiday destination, having decided which island is most suitable Invite a friend.

- Review the first chapter.
- Write two more chapters.
  REWARD: Buy an outfit for the book publicity tour.

Some of the rewards are personal and some feed into her goal of writing a novel. Carmella had to display discipline in writing the book, and the rewards were of her own choosing. What she didn't realise at the beginning was that even after her novel was published, it was likely to take twelve months before she had any real sales figures for it. That's why it is important to reward yourself when the book is published, because it all fades steadily after that day.

Carmella has since completed her novel, and it's in the editing process. She will keep refining it until her editor tells her it shines. At that point, she knows it will be time to approach publishers.

What goals do you have, and what rewards will you give yourself for realising them? The exercise below may help you answer those questions.

REWARDS FOR GOALS EXERCISE

- Name a goal you seek to achieve.

- What small steps (in natural order) need to be taken?

- Choose a suitable reward for realising your goal.

- Schedule several smaller rewards you'll need to motivate you along the way.

- Insert these smaller rewards after each important step on the path to your goal.

- Place this outline where you can see it regularly.

- If your goal is the purchase of something, go out and view the object that will be your reward.

- Take the first step on the path to your goal.

CHAPTER NINETEEN

Anchoring the Feeling

When your long-term aims are far from your present position, you may need to experience something of that yearned-for goal, in order to feel what it will be like to achieve it. If, for example, your goal is to live in a grand old home with a large garden, perhaps it's time for you to spend a night or two in a grand old home.

This might mean staying a few nights in a mansion that has been converted to a private hotel. After breakfast in the morning, you'll be free to stroll around the grounds, explore the gardens, read a book in the sunroom, stare out to sea on one of the verandahs or to sketch the ducks on the pond. As you absorb the sights, the sounds, the smells and the ambience of a grand old home, you'll be forming a mental picture, a feeling, and auditory memories of what your goal might be like when you reach it.

Making your goal as real and as solid as possible helps you to have a point of focus. You are less likely to be thrown off balance by life.

In classes, this is demonstrated by having all the students stand up and stretch out their arms. Then, keeping their arms outstretched to the sides, they are asked to lift a leg, so that they are standing on one leg only. Next they are required to stand on their toes on that one leg. Most of them fall over within ten seconds.

Afterwards, it is explained how ballet dancers manage to turn around five or more times in a row without becoming dizzy or falling. It's called spotting. As the dancers prepare to pirouette, they fix their gaze on an identifiable spot on the wall, or on the curtain or even on a member of the audience. Each time they turn around and return to this point, they have that same spot to act as their point of focus. Students are then asked to pick a point on the wall, fix their gaze on it, stand on one leg with arms outstretched again, and then step up onto the toes of that foot. Most of them make it past ten seconds this time.

Having a point of focus in your life is very similar. You can use it to tell you when you are off centre in the pursuit of your goal. This works very well with physical goals, but how do you spot a goal that is emotional? Unless you have experienced the feeling you are trying to develop, it may be difficult to know if you are approaching it.

Perhaps the simplest way to know the feeling you desire to build in your life is to complete the Underlying Needs exercise below. (This exercise first appeared in my book *A Secret Door to the Universe*, Simon & Schuster Australia, 1999, p.57) and it is employed here again because it applies to both spiritual and emotional basic needs. It is a simple exercise and best written down so that you can review it a week after completing it. You'll probably be surprised at how little you actually need, and at how complicated you have made your life in the pursuit of one simple need.

UNDERLYING NEEDS EXERCISE

- What do you most want in your life right now?

- What would you get from having it ?

Keep asking yourself these questions until you come to a simple feeling. In my years of observing how clients and students complete this exercise, I have noted that their answers lead to only two final responses: peace and stillness. Even these two are close to being one answer.

The next two examples illustrate this point. The first case is Dino, who wanted to be rich.

He explained that wealth would bring him power and then added that from a position of power, he'd have control over his life. He further explained that, with control, he'd have fewer surprises, increasing his happiness. From more happiness, he'd derive more peace.

Peace was Dino's ultimate goal, and he had chosen a demanding career to earn big money in order to gain greater control over his life and have fewer surprises, which would bring more inner peace.

He was then asked the following questions:

- Is this the shortest path to inner peace for you?

- Is this the most appropriate path to your goal of inner peace?

- Can you describe another viable path to inner peace that you might take?

- Which, if any, steps on your current path hinder the pursuit of your goal of inner peace?

Dino wasn't asked to change the path to his desired goal, only to examine it. He was also challenged to examine other possible routes. This was so that he might either decide that his path was indeed the best or that he should look at alternatives.

Clients usually know what they want deep down — all they need is careful prompting. In less than ten questions, Dino discovered his deeper needs. He pondered the possible routes to it for a few weeks and returned with questions on how he might change his path. He wanted a simpler one, now aware that all the stress of the high-powered job was not leading him to inner peace.

The second example involved Teresa, who wanted her own home. At 35 years of age, she was tired of sharing rented houses with strangers. She had some wild stories to tell of experiences in shared households. Being single, it wasn't a straightforward case of moving in with a partner or securing a loan together and buying a house.

Teresa had been saving for almost five years but, in that period, house prices had risen by around 35 per cent in the areas in which she had been looking to buy. She was despondent by the time she consulted me. In effect, Teresa had a purpose and a goal: to own a home. I asked her what she'd get from having her own home.

Clients usually know what they want deep down – all they need is careful prompting.

'I can plant whatever I want in the garden and paint the walls any colour I choose. I'm sick of landlord cream.'

'Landlord cream?'

'Yes, it's not technically a paint-chart colour, but it ought to be. Every house I've lived in has been painted that bland cream. I'm certain that landlords get a job-lot discount.'

'What might you get from painting the walls as you wish and planting things in the garden?'

'I'd have a sense that all my efforts at work were going towards something worthwhile.'

'What might you derive from that sense that your efforts were going towards something worthwhile?'

'I'd be happier, and I wouldn't care about all the work politics.'

'What might being happier and no longer caring about the work politics do for you?'

'I'd be able to come home and know that the house is as I left it in the morning.'

'What might you get from coming home knowing that the house was as you left it in the morning?'

'Security.'

'And what might security do for you?'

'Give me peace of mind.'

'So your bottom line appears to be peace of mind. Is that right?'

'Yes. Yes, it is, now that I think about it.'

'So is a house your ticket to peace of mind?'

'Yes,' she replied quietly, feeling overwhelmed by the realisation.

'So if you're not currently in a relationship, and you have no partner with whom you can purchase a house, what other alternatives are there for you?'

'I can keep saving for a bigger deposit.'

'Yes, but by your own admission, house prices are increasing faster than you can save. What other choices might you have?'

'I can buy a unit, but I don't want a unit. I want to have my own garden.'

'What other choices might there be?'

'I can ask my sister to go in with me. She mentioned last month that she is thinking about buying a place. She doesn't have much of a deposit saved, but she has a well-paid job.'

'What other choices are there?'

'I might ask my parents to go in with me on the loan, but without contributing to the initial deposit. I can then rent out a room to cover the payments. And when I sell the place, I can get the next loan in my own name.'

'That sounds good to me. What other choices are there?'

'I can move interstate where houses are cheaper, and then I can afford a place by myself.'

'That sounds viable. What other choices are there?'

The process with Teresa took several sessions, during which time she recognised that her job was stressing her more than she wanted. She changed jobs, earning more money in the new position. Her parents agreed to put their names on her home loan, so that she was able to purchase a house. She is sharing it with a friend, to cover the payments. She's probably living in a brightly coloured house with a garden crammed with flowers and plants. Teresa deserves the peace she seeks.

Having completed the first part of the exercise for yourself, it's time for you to complete the second part. On the same piece of paper, answer these questions:

- Is this the shortest path to inner peace for you?

- Is this the most appropriate way to your goal of inner peace?

- Is there another viable route that you might take?

- Which, if any, steps on your current path hinder your pursuit of your goal of inner peace?

More often than not, we pursue a tangible goal and end up with a feeling. It's one path of many. We have only to decide if it is the most appropriate one for us.

So, in your pursuit of fulfilment, maybe a job leads to a boat, which steers you towards a girlfriend, and this relationship offers shared experiences that bring happiness, which means fulfilment. It's often more complicated than this, but there is an obvious pattern.

Are your goals leading you towards your purpose? What purpose do they lead you towards?

CHAPTER TWENTY

Differentiating Between Goals and Purpose

Sometimes it can be difficult to determine whether you are pursuing a goal or your purpose. Perhaps the definition below may help you to decide.

Goals are what you want from life, whereas purpose is what you give back to the world.

To know your purpose, you need to understand your innate qualities, in order to know what you can give back to the world.

Chances are, if you have completed both parts of the exercise in the previous chapter, you have an awareness of your deepest underlying need. You're most likely also aware of the physical goals you have selected in pursuit of your emotional and spiritual purpose.

Are the emotional and spiritual needs and the physical goals in harmony with one another or in conflict? If, for instance, you have stillness as your deepest need, and you have a competitive, demanding lifestyle as one of your goals, how does this goal bring you closer to your underlying need? Without tossing your lifestyle aside, can you make a few small changes that will make it more compatible with your deeper need? If not, is it necessary to reassess your chosen path to that goal?

If you recognise your underlying need and fulfil it, your life purpose is more likely to become clear to you. This is why it is most important for you to be aware of the path you are treading and the underlying need you want to meet.

A friend who recently heard about this book laughed cynically at talk of goals and purpose. 'These are the questions you are asked when applying for a job. Interviewers always want to know what you want from life and where you see yourself in five years' time. Just for once, I'd like to reply that I want to be running the company in five years and also be the major shareholder, but only if I can work just fifteen hours per week.'

Interviewers probably ask these questions to see if the candidate will suit the company culture, but the potential employee might well ask the interviewer and the CEO the same questions. They are important questions for each of us to put to ourselves periodically. More than the brief and often all-too-hasty resolutions we make on or around the first of January each year, we need to ask ourselves these questions to ensure our lives have direction. To do this effectively, we have to know our underlying needs.

If we ignore them, all the success in the world won't fulfil us. Hollow victories abound, but such victories do not lead to fulfilment, or to a sense of purpose. It's like winning back $20 of the $35 you've just fed into a poker machine.

The deepest purpose is what humankind has been searching for since time began. It is the question with which religions, spiritual groups and philosophic organisations have been grappling for centuries. It is encapsulated in these three questions:

- Where did we come from?

- Why are we here?

• Where are we ultimately heading?

There are dozens of answers to each of these questions, and each is correct to those who accept it. They are simple questions, but they can take years to answer with any sense of personal certainty.

Some argue that they have discovered the true meaning of existence, while others suggest that existence only has the meaning we give to it. In the case of the first question, 'Where did we come from?' the evidence is limited for proving beyond reasonable doubt any belief in our origins.

In answer to the question 'Why are we here?', if it is true that life only has the meaning we give it, this is a tremendous opportunity. What meaning do you want to give your life? To what purpose do you want to devote the remainder of your years here?

In response to the question 'Where are we ultimately heading?' very little of our long-term future can be proven while still living, and the deceased seem reluctant to return to tell us about it. The only question or period over which we have any control is the present time, so that brings us back to this lifetime. If you wanted to devote your life to a particular purpose, what purpose might you choose? Assuming that you arrived with a sense of purpose, how can you remember what you are here to do?

Dahlia described a meditation regression she experienced in the 1980s when she was guided back to the day of her birth. The purpose was to determine what sort of beginning she'd had, and what decisions she might have made about life and her family on day one. Although it is difficult to determine the accuracy of such regressions, Dahlia was surprised at the reaction she had when her father visited the hospital. Becoming aware of his presence, she decided that this was a man likely to wreak havoc during her formative years. She also decided that if she wanted to have a good life, she'd have to commence it after leaving the house of that man. If that was, indeed, her first reaction to her father, it proved correct.

It may be necessary to differentiate between goals and purpose. Goals are end results, whereas purpose continues after we have achieved it.

While you may have happiness as your goal, once you achieve a state of happiness you have realised your goal. It is unlikely that you'll continually remain in a state of happiness; being happy becomes a purpose. Buying a home and winning an award are also goals, whereas improving the welfare of others can be perceived as a purpose, because after it has been attained, it needs to be maintained.

A simpler way to differentiate between the two is to look at career. If you ask, 'What is your line of work?' you are asking about career and associated goals. If you ask, 'What is your life's work', you may be asking about something that has no relation to a job or to income. A person's lifework may be the preservation of a species of butterfly, or the provision of safe drinking water to villages in Third World countries. Lifework can include, but is not limited to, the following:

- Raising healthy, well-adjusted children.

- Providing a safe framework for financial stability in the community.

- Teaching others to be more than they have been.

- Entertaining people to help them forget their troubles, even if only for a few minutes.

- Healing the sick.

- Hearing those who are ignored by society.

- Discovering new medicines.

- Teaching the lessons of history.

- Helping others to make sense of life.

- Supporting someone who is a leader in their field.

- Fighting for a cause.

- Helping others, through books or films, to escape the drudgery of their lives.

- Reminding others of the need to feed the spirit.

- Growing healthy wholesome food to feed the community.

- Protecting the community or the country.

- Mediating between groups that are antagonistic towards each other.

- Showing others what humans are capable of achieving.

The list is infinite, but one thing stands out. It is possible that purpose is sometimes found through those experiences that are most emotionally intense or which have caused us the most pain in the past.

A relevant example was recently described by a friend. She mentioned how her partner, a volunteer fireman, was standing around one afternoon talking with other firemen and volunteers when someone asked if anyone present had ever caused a fire. All the hands went up. Some had accidentally lit fires. Others were more aware of their intentions. This probably makes back-burning an exciting and longed-for event in their yearly calendar.

It's common for students of clairvoyance and psychic development to have a fear of the future, which they hope will be resolved through their studies. Another example of the past shaping purpose is the British actor Richard Griffiths, whose diction is remarkably clear and precise. Both his parents were profoundly deaf. It is entirely possible that this fact led him to value speech more than most of us.

What incidents stand out from your past as painful or emotionally intense? How have they shaped your life? Have they given you a sense of purpose or increased it within you?

Once you have identified your purpose, how do you remember it in everyday life? How do you keep from forgetting it in the rush to earn and spend and live in the physical world?

An example of how issues from childhood can fashion within us a sense of purpose occurred with Dominic, a solidly built man who explained over a snack how he came to own a popular restaurant.

'I grew up in a family of eight children, and we were very poor,' he said as he topped up our wine glasses. 'No matter how much my mother cooked it seems that I was always hungry. The other kids, too. I learned that if I helped her with the groceries, I'd have first grab at the weekly food baskets. It was a bit sneaky but I figured that I'd earned it through carrying those heavy baskets home twice a week. It didn't matter how much I carried, it was all gone within a day or two. I vowed as a boy that when I grew up I'd never be without food again. In fact I felt it my duty to see that those here in the village have enough to eat, too. So now I run my own restaurant, and it's nearly always full. In an hour or two this place will be filled with hungry people, coming here to be fed and to leave happy. In the summer they line up out there in the street for a table.'

The hunger from childhood had left its mark, and instead of being greedy for food, Dominic had instead realised that if he was frequently hungry, so too must others be hungry. He is still providing food for those around him, but instead of staggering home with heavily laden baskets twice a week, he is receiving deliveries and overseeing the kitchen. He derives a deep sense of fulfilment from providing inexpensive yet tasty food for the locals.

He must be doing something right because later that evening there wasn't a spare table to be seen in the restaurant and Dominic was chatting away to patrons as though they were visiting him in his own home.

CHAPTER TWENTY-ONE

Remembering Purpose Daily

Once you have identified your life's purpose, you'll need to remind yourself of your purpose regularly. All of us have experienced the sudden insight that seemed astoundingly important, but which was later forgotten. The same can be said for ideas.

A friend named Douglas, who is a clairvoyant, told me of his idea for a book entitled *How Clairvoyant Is That?!* The first chapter was entitled, 'I knew you'd buy this book'. Douglas comes up with these ideas on a weekly basis, and he used to forget them with the same ease with which he conceived them. Now he remembers them by writing them all down. He wants to write under the pseudonym 'Madame Hildegard of the immaculate perception'.

When you have powerful insights into your life's purpose, you'll need to set up reminders to ensure you stay on the path. Reminders can take many forms:

- Write them down in a diary.

- Leave a note somewhere very visible — on your computer or the fridge door.

- Meditate on a daily basis.

- Meditate each week with a group (for group support).

- Attend spiritual gatherings.

- Attend events with those who share your purpose.

- Dreams at night as a reminder from your subconscious mind.

- Read books to refresh your awareness of your purpose.

- Put up a photograph or a poster that reminds you of your purpose.

Inertia is sometimes the greatest obstacle in the battle to pursue purpose. Having discovered your purpose and taken the first tentative steps towards fulfilling it, you find that life distracts you from it. When I have a client who is too lazy or unmotivated to take the first steps towards purpose or a goal, I remind them that they have to live with the annoyance and frustration that accompanies such inertia. I point out that the goal they desire will probably be realised by someone else, and not necessarily as well as they could have realised it.

Instead of being overwhelmed by the enormity of a goal or the pursuit of a purpose, limit your view to the short-term and to the steps you can take today. If you take one small step each day towards your purpose, in three years you'll have taken over a thousand steps.

Where once you may have had passion to immerse yourself in your purpose, your addiction to goals and short-term achievements now seems to demand more of your time, attention and energy. This leaves you limited resources for the pursuit of purpose.

Perhaps at the end of a hectic day, you cannot concentrate on a book, you may have no energy left to attend an event with those who share your purpose or you fall asleep as you attempt to meditate.

What has happened? You have allowed your goals — or worse, the goals others have set for you — to crowd in on your purpose. Those daily habits can eat away a whole lifetime, if you allow them to.

If you take one small step each day towards your purpose, in three years you'll have taken over a thousand steps.

When you cannot find the discipline or the way to restructure your life in order to make room for your purpose, you may need to pay someone else to do this for you.

That can mean consulting a counsellor, taking meditation classes or courses in whatever your purpose involves. It may require that you consult a life coach or someone who'll help you to restructure your life, and who will keep you on track until you have established new behaviour patterns. I suggest paying strangers to help you as they may have less invested in your remaining the same. I'm not suggesting that your friends or family don't have your best interests at heart, but they have their own needs and agendas, and your decision to change your life may hinder their plans.

An example of this occurred with Veronique, whose decision to meditate wasn't part of her family's agenda. Each afternoon when she shut herself away in her bedroom to meditate for 20 minutes, one family member after another decided this was the best time to tell her about something, ask where a pair of shoes might be, mention a phone call, etc.

Veronique patiently explained that anything, including news of the death of a loved one or a lottery win, was to wait until she had completed her daily meditation. Her family did stop entering her room as she meditated, but they didn't give up their subconscious need to distract her from her time alone. Her husband started a power saw outside the window one afternoon, while on another occasion her son took to bouncing a basketball against the side of the house. On still another day, her thirteen-year-old daughter decided to play some CDs and then had to shout over the noise when her friend rang to chat.

Veronique was determined. At first she allowed them a few weeks to become familiar with the new routine of 20 minutes without contact each afternoon, but eventually she offered them a choice. She told them all that either they were to allow her those 20 minutes of undisturbed peace or she'd drive off to meditate somewhere else. With a 30-minute drive each way and perhaps a 20-minute stop for a drink or a sandwich, she'd be gone almost two hours each day. The choice was theirs: 20 minutes or two hours of no contact every day.

To keep yourself on track daily, it pays to ask yourself the following questions:

- What have I done today towards my goals?

- What will I do tomorrow towards realising my goals?

- What have I done today towards fulfilling my purpose?

- What will I do tomorrow towards the fulfilment of my purpose?

CHAPTER TWENTY-TWO

Direct Experience Shapes Your Purpose

It is important to continually differentiate between goals and purpose. Sometimes the mundane goals we set for ourselves steal our sense of purpose by crowding in on our valuable time and demanding all of our attention.

Developing the habit of pausing to reflect upon your day or your week can help. It offers you the chance to see if your goals have taken you towards your purpose or away from it. Both are necessary for a fulfilling life. The fundamental difference is that the fulfilment from pursuing your purpose lasts longer than the fulfilment from realising your goals.

Those who have experienced the excitement which comes from purchasing a new car, a motorbike, a boat, a wide-screen TV or even a high-tech appliance know that this feeling wears off in time. For some it wears off the moment they unsuccessfully attempt to assemble or operate the new appliance while for others it fades over the next few weeks or months. Realising your purpose can give you this excitement every day, as there are many different ways to realise the same purpose. If your purpose is to help others to laugh in order that they might forget their burdens for a while, then you'll probably experience joy with each new funny idea or joke you invent or discover. Your purpose continues beyond each small or large goal, giving you joy along the way.

Travis's story is relevant. His goal was to be a successful musician, whereas his purpose was to raise a family differently from the way he had been raised. Since his childhood, Travis has wanted to play music, but his parents had felt that music was trivial and not a proper career for their son. They had pushed him towards engineering instead.

As soon as Travis was old enough to leave home, he did. This allowed him to chart his own course in life. He played in bands and wrote a few songs, living the life he had dreamed of. Eventually, he settled into a combination of part-time work in the mainstream and part-time work as a musician.

Now in his forties, Travis still plays professionally three evenings each week. He is fulfilling his goal of earning an income from music. He has two sons, of whom he is justifiably proud. His purpose involves raising his sons to be whatever they want to be. One of his sons wants to be an engineer, which echoes his grandfather's need for stability and security. The other boy has no idea what he wants to do, and Travis feels that he is providing him with a platform to explore life and his own purpose.

Travis has found a way to realise his goals and pursue his purpose at the same time. This balance is often an essential part of a fulfilling life. It is rarely necessary to be a martyr to your purpose or to have to sacrifice all your goals and desires for it — unless those goals conceal or distract you from your purpose. Travis has had opportunities to travel interstate and overseas with his work as a musician, but he has limited his time away from the children, as he values his family life, realising that it feeds him both emotionally and spiritually.

Sometimes we equate purpose with a quest that is larger than life, whereas in reality, it is difficult to measure what you give back to the world. In the case of Travis, he doesn't know how much his efforts to raise independent, open-minded children will impact on the generations after him.

The size of the quest is not as important as the fact that you pursue it. Your purpose feeds you as much as your goals do, even though you are giving back to life instead of seeking something from it, as is the case when you are pursuing your goals. While some have a purpose that changes lives or alters the course of history, the smaller, less visible purpose pursued by most of us is no less important.

Almost everyone can recall a teacher from school or university who inspired the thirst for knowledge. Perhaps that teacher aroused a lifelong interest in a subject? It might be that he or she taught you in an unusual way or showed you what you were capable of doing, achieving or understanding.

Teachers are paid to teach, but when they illuminate a subject or pay special attention to the learning needs of a student, they are giving more than they are paid to do. If you are a teacher and teaching is your life's purpose, each time you give more than is asked of your role, you receive in return. It can be truly rewarding to watch a student grasp an idea and experiment with it.

When you consider that someone (or several people) taught Einstein mathematics, Mozart the piano and Shakespeare writing, you can see how a person's purpose encourages others to pursue their own purpose as scientists, musicians, playwrights, etc.

Following true purpose, you'll derive sufficient fulfilment from pursuing it, however simple it may seem to others. You may have to balance the pursuit of your purpose with the daily demands of life.

Purpose became clear to me as I wrote my astrology book. In the section on the Moon's nodes, I found that a person's date of birth revealed one of the lessons they had come to learn. Mine was to break problems into puzzles and to make those puzzles appealing to others, so that they might tackle them and solve their own problems.

That is what this book is about. Enjoying a purposeful life is the desire of many people, yet sometimes goals get in the way of purpose. I can't stress enough that if you can find a balance between your goals and your purpose, life can be very rewarding.

In discerning what we can give back to the world, many of us consider our strengths or qualities for a clue. In some cases, the reverse is essential. If we look at our issues, problems and weaknesses, we find the things we need to master before we can proceed purposefully through life.

In mastering those weaknesses or issues, we strengthen ourselves. We are then in a position to assist others to resolve those same or similar weaknesses or issues, based on our first-hand experience.

As I encounter an issue, I turn it into a puzzle. When I solve the puzzle, I can then apply that puzzle-solving method to similar issues or problems. It doesn't work in every case, therefore I'm forced to find new methods.

An example of this process occurred with a client named Hamish, who worked in a large corporation. The corporation decided to cut staff numbers. Hearing about this, Hamish studied the business and came up with an idea that might earn it healthy profits in return for a small outlay. As a result, when the axe came down and Hamish's entire section was made redundant, he was left standing. Over the next two years, he continually found new projects and presented them to those at the top. They financed some of them. He remained employed, despite not having anyone to report to — no supervisor, section or even divisional manager.

No-one quite knew what Hamish's role was. As long as he came up with new ideas and secured finance from one of the directors, he remained well paid. While those around him had seen the staff cuts as a threat to their jobs, Hamish had seen a puzzle. 'How can I remain employed with this organisation?' he had asked himself. He has answered that question in over ten different ways throughout the past two years. Each project continues his employment.

There are often many more solutions to a problem or a puzzle than the ones we find. We tend to stick with the first solution, happy that we have arrived at an answer. It's not surprising that those who have conquered alcohol or drugs make the best teachers about the perils of substance abuse. Direct experience often contributes to finding and pursuing purpose.

CHAPTER TWENTY-THREE

Guidance Along the Path

Having identified your purpose, it is important to be reminded of the path from time to time. Beyond this, it is sometimes essential to have some guidance when the path becomes obscure or diverges into several directions.

Two ways to pursue your purpose and be guided towards the best alternatives when choices are presented are the group way and the individual way. Each has its benefits and its drawbacks. A blend of both is often a successful formula.

THE GROUP PATH

- Includes support groups;

- allows you to share experiences with others who are pursuing the same purpose;

- offers living role models through teachers or fellow group members;

- can demand that you conform to the group's expectations;

- can teach you negative behaviour patterns;

- can lead you towards a more acceptable path, which may not be precisely your own path.

THE INDIVIDUAL PATH

- Allows you the freedom to make your own way at your own pace;

- allows you to discover things first-hand;

- offers living and deceased role models, through books or courses;

- allows you a unique approach to your purpose;

- can leave you feeling unsupported when you need it;

- offers you total responsibility for fulfilling your purpose.

Different paths suit different people. Stuart grew up in a country town. He wanted to become an actor, but was too afraid to take lessons, for fear of what his friends and schoolmates might say. When he moved to a large city at the age of nineteen, he decided to take acting lessons.

Delighted to find many like-minded people studying with him, he made new friends and soon had a support network when he wanted to practise outside the classroom or attend a performance. One of his new friends, Alice, had a small practice room at home, and together they improved their skills, reading from favourite plays day and night.

The group path suited Stuart because it offered him a chance to feel normal amongst people who loved what he loved. He also found positive role models at the acting school, in teachers, more advanced students and professional actors who had trained at the school previously. The group path also offered Stuart structure, knowledge, friendships, and competition to improve his abilities.

In contrast, the individual path was preferred by Fiona, whose meditation practices suited her need for solitude and reflection. Although she worked at a full-time job, Fiona managed to meditate every day.

Preferring to keep her two-bedroom apartment to herself, she used the spare room for meditation. It was sparsely furnished, the way she liked it. Each morning at 5:30, she'd light a candle and sit on her cushion to meditate for an hour.

In meditation she asked for advice from those parts of her which knew the answers and, more often than not, she was able to glimpse the consequences of her decisions and actions before she committed herself to a particular direction. In this way, Fiona was able to pursue her purpose and receive inner guidance to keep her on track. Although some people might find this a lonely path, Fiona was content with it, as she felt less likely to be thrown off centre by the ideas and opinions of others.

Both paths offer opportunities and yet each path has its restrictions. You probably won't need to debate the pros and cons of these paths as you'll find yourself naturally drawn to one or the other. Generally, independent self-motivated people prefer the individual path, whereas those who are more social and who value a sense of community or belonging prefer the group path.

CHAPTER TWENTY-FOUR

Emergency Exit

Why do we need emergency exits? For some it is to avoid the 'big C' (Commitment) while for others, they never commit to something without having an exit clause. For most of us, however, emergency exits are useful when life becomes too burdensome.

An example of this occurred with a friend who arrived at my door looking like an emotional wreck. Byron had been retrenched from his job, had surrendered his car because he couldn't afford the repayments and had lost many of his fair-weather friends because he was unable to afford their lifestyle. I knew immediately that he didn't want platitudes such as 'the darkest hour is just before the storm' or 'every cloud has a silver lining'. He wanted to forget his life, if only for a while.

We sat by the open fire, I pressed a glass of liqueur into one hand and a fire poker into the other. Byron drained his glass and began adjusting the logs for more warmth. We talked about dozens of things, keeping well clear of his finances and his work situation. An hour later we were laughing as we recalled some of the ridiculous things we had done in the past, in the hope of finding happiness, as we ate and drank. As the sun set, we sat beside a fire which grew too hot for comfort. Instead of allowing it to die down, we simply moved our chairs back and discarded our jackets. As I loaded a log onto the already high pile I heard Byron state: 'There's always room for one more log, isn't there?' We reclined talking and laughing as sparks shot out across the floor, overshooting the hearth rug and smouldering on the carpet. I was silently congratulating myself on being a reliable emergency exit when a mutual friend, Samantha, knocked at the door. After striding towards the open fire she turned to Byron and said, 'Byron, what's wrong? You look awful.' The emergency exit was gone and Byron was suddenly aware of his issues again.

An emergency exit can take the form of a cricket match, a workout at the gym, a weekend away in the country to maintain your sanity or a meal composed of all those foods you have given up due to allergies or the need to reduce weight. It has been previously mentioned that you know when you are following your purpose by how fulfilled you feel. Let's consider the reverse.

How do you know when you are not pursuing your purpose? Sometimes we are afraid to commit ourselves fully to one direction in case we are wrong or it leads to a dead end. To protect ourselves, we may want to look at exit strategies in the event of needing a suitable exit. The problem is that while building the exit road, we risk using it.

Rosa had this experience. Her rich fantasy life made up for her drab mundane existence. She fell in love regularly, but not necessarily with the intent of pursuing a relationship. She often secretly desired those around her, fantasising about how life might be with them.

Instead of putting her energy where it might do some good, Rosa sought refuge in her imagination. Yet, when she came for a consultation, she was unable to pinpoint why she felt chronically depressed.

'Perhaps the depression is a reminder that you are not pursuing your real purpose here,' I suggested. Over the following weeks, she agreed to block off her exits, one by one, by acknowledging that the men she fantasised about were not interested in a relationship with her. As she examined each exit or fantasy, she recognised how they were keeping her impotent, away from reality.

When she had only one fantasy exit left, she was on shaky ground indeed, as she had to face the reality that her life was miserable. It is important to have at least one exit in case things go wrong, so Rosa left the last one and worked on becoming powerful and centred in her present-day life.

Eventually her daily life blossomed, as she grew accustomed to living in the present, with the opportunities she was actually able to pursue. Then something unexpected occurred. Rosa decided that she didn't actually want a love relationship, as she felt that it might compromise her new life. She was so filled with purpose that she feared a man might take her from it. She was afraid that she might sink back into fantasy again.

It is possible to slip back, but when you've been continuously present and powerful in your own life for a period of time, people can rarely dissuade you from your purpose. It was a long and arduous process for Rosa, but she was prepared to ignore her exit and push on towards her purpose. She was beginning to reap the rewards of her efforts when a man arrived wanting a love relationship with her.

'He's a nice guy, but such a dreamer,' she said. 'He has his head in the clouds most of the time, which I find irritating.' She was on the path.

A different exit strategy was employed by Stefan, whose drinking was driving his family away as well as ruining his health. Stefan felt that he'd had his 'one chance' to pursue his purpose and had messed it up.

It is not uncommon to find people who believe in the 'One Chance' formula for life. From an early age, we are told stories about the one chance for love in fables such as 'Sleeping Beauty', and we are continually asked, 'What will you be when you grow up?' — as though when we mature, we stagnate. I now believe that the correct answer for children asked that question is simply 'bigger'.

Stefan had wanted his own business and had purchased a bakery. Three years later the business collapsed, leaving Stefan with a mountain of debt that took him over five years to repay. During this five-year period, he often compared himself with friends who were doing well financially, and it depressed him. Drinking anaesthetised the pain, so he drank regularly. His drinking habits also took away his family, his ability to earn a living and his health.

Because of the exit road Stefan had taken, his goal of financial independence and his purpose became a distant memory. Exit roads are necessary but, if taken, it is only a matter of time before you have to return to the freeway, to your purpose, again.

There are a great many ways to escape purpose. One involved Glenda and Omid, who were struggling financially. They had periods without work, and the bills kept arriving. Omid busied himself around their country property, keeping his hands active but not earning any money, while Glenda stayed inside, staring at the unpaid bills.

Eventually she decided that to cheer herself up, she'd take the family out to dinner, courtesy of her credit card. During previous low periods this had given everyone a sense of wellbeing, and Glenda felt confident it might help again. That evening they agreed on a restaurant in a nearby town, dressed up and set off. The meal was expensive, but it served to make Glenda, Omid and the family feel worthwhile, as they settled in for a sumptuous and sensual experience.

Reality struck home when the whole family suffered food poisoning for two days because of something they had eaten at the restaurant. The meal had not yet been paid for and it had certainly not cheered them up. Instead, it had laid them all low, as the bills continued arriving. Glenda has since set a goal of eliminating her debts and improving her financial position.

Financial outlays can make us feel in control of our lives when we are stuck, unable to move forward towards our goals or our purpose. We spend up in order to have all the trappings — and that's exactly what happens: we are trapped until we pay for the things we have purchased. Even if we do pay for them outright, we still have to maintain and repair them.

A friend mentioned an overseas stay that revealed to her how little she actually needed for a fulfilling life. She was holidaying in Australia from the UK with her partner and rented a cheap, partly furnished house, close to the beach, so that she might swim in the ocean each morning and evening.

Pia explained that they had a simple philosophy regarding furniture and kitchen equipment: 'If you can't see it, we don't have it. If we don't have it, we don't need it.' They arrived for a six-month stay with two suitcases and spent around $200 on basic cooking utensils, groceries and a lamp. Friends soon contributed a few bits and pieces, and local garage sales provided more. They had a spartan house and a full life.

A holiday house is not the same as a permanent home. In the former, you aren't ironing clothes for work, or working from home, etc. Yet a yearly garage sale of your own might reveal to you how much you buy and then throw away.

If you take the spending exit from the freeway to your purpose, you may soon find yourself mired in debt. This can take years to discharge, before you can actively pursue more meaningful goals and your purpose.

Samantha took a different exit: her need to be loved and needed took her away from completing her studies in psychology. With less than a year to go to complete a six-year degree, Samantha met Fabian, who wanted her to stay at home and cook for him. She abandoned her studies and learned to cook the dishes he loved. She argues that pleasing him is her purpose, but the spiritually hungry and tired look she has developed suggests that Fabian is the only one being fed by their relationship.

Next time you feel stuck in your life, or you feel that you are making no progress towards your goals or your purpose, notice what you do. Take note of which exit you use to get immediate gratification.

In an age where instant fulfilment is the acceptable norm, some goals still require effort, courage, commitment and time. The worthwhile things, such as meaningful goals and life purpose, are worth the time and effort, for their rewards last longer than most instant gratification.

EXIT STRATEGY EXERCISE

- What exit strategies do you have in place for when you feel frustrated or unable to pursue your goals or purpose?

- How often do you use these exits?

- Do you use them when you might be better off approaching your goals from a different perspective?

- Is escape from reality through dreams and imagination one of your emergency exits?

- Do you regularly escape through any of the following?
  Gambling
  Sex or short-term love affairs
  Work or career commitments
  Hoping for divine intervention
  Drugs or alcohol
  Self-pity

Looking back over the last five years, how have you dealt with prolonged periods of frustration? What exit can you put into place that will serve you well when frustrations engulf you in the future?

CHAPTER TWENTY-FIVE

The Bigger Picture

To lend some perspective to goals and purpose, we need to examine the bigger picture. The exercise below is designed to help you see where you are on the path of this lifetime. Take a pen and paper and complete it without lingering too long on any one question. Sometimes greater accuracy comes from answers that simply fly out of your mouth or pen.

- Off the top of your head, what age do you expect to live to?

- How old are you now?

- According to your answer to the first question, what percentage of your life have you lived so far?

- What percentage of your life is left?

- What has been the main theme of your life so far?

- What do you want the main theme of the rest of your life to be?

- Are you presently working towards this theme?

- If not, what can you do to begin?

Examining the theme of your life until now can be a powerful eye-opener. In workshops it is not uncommon to hear words like pain, struggle, obligations, responsibilities and misery used to describe the themes of participants' lives.

Pop songs sometimes capture the essence of a life or relationship. This was illustrated in Adam's story. His five-year relationship with Rebekka ran to the theme of the Beatles song 'Girl'. It's a song about the girl who came to stay and then took over the life of the man, directing him towards what would make her happy. Adam explained how that became his theme song, especially at the end of their relationship.

Perhaps he needs to select a more sanguine Beatles song for his next relationship — to avoid having the song 'Yesterday' as his next theme …

A simple way to gain a clear perspective on the process of your life in terms of years is to draw a bar chart of it. The process is as follows:

- Decide how many years you think you will experience this lifetime.

- Divide the decades of your life into sections.

- Colour in the part you have already lived, and then hold the page up.

- See for yourself how much of your life has passed, and how much you believe you have left.

Tears often result when clients complete this exercise, as they realise how much time they have already spent in pursuit of goals that have not fulfilled them. Some clients reach for excuses, such as family responsibilities, lack of financial support or lack of education. All of these can be genuine impediments to the pursuit of goals and the realisation of purpose, but they cannot erase the years already spent. They can be assets, however, serving to motivate you to move forward more rapidly towards your goals and purpose. This occurred with Angela, whose father controlled the family through money.

When she left home, Angela was determined not to be controlled by a man, especially financially. Soon she was in a relationship with Alfonso, who was twelve years older and had devoted most of his life to working hard and earning money.

Angela gradually realised that she was replicating her relationship with her father. Alfonso controlled their finances completely. He owned both cars, the house and the furniture. Every time she wanted to buy something or do anything costing money, she had to justify her needs to Alfonso. She seemed to have stepped into a love relationship that repeated her childhood role models.

Most of us repeat family patterns. Some of us do it continuously. In Angela's case, she knew that to be free she had to earn her own income, which would allow her to make her own decisions. She commenced working and saving money to rent a home of her own. Motivated by the memories of how her mother had been a prisoner to her father, she studied at night after work, in order to secure a better job.

Having left the relationship, Angela has had to work at not repeating it with other men. Fighting her parental relationship patterns, she was able to find other female role models who offered a more assertive and independent path to emulate.

Glimpsing the bigger picture of where you are in your life can assist you in reassessing your direction. Initiating change with the bigger picture in mind helps to keep you on course. You'll still have to take care of all the smaller decisions and changes in direction, of course, as these may prevent you from pursuing your purpose.

Becoming aware of the bigger picture can remind you of where you are heading. It is often obscured by the daily demands of life. These and the decisions you make are likely to become your life. If you focus entirely on the daily demands, and you live for 70 years, you'll experience daily choices on more than 25,550 days. On how many of those days will you remember your purpose? While it is important to view your path without judgment or blame, it is important to avoid the pitfalls of becoming lost in the daily distractions and demands of life.

Becoming aware of the bigger picture can remind you of where you are heading.

When you keep the bigger picture in mind it becomes apparent that your life is developing a theme. If you don't like the theme of your life so far, you need to make immediate efforts to change it. Keeping an awareness of life's bigger picture helps you to remember that you are not guaranteed fulfilment in this lifetime, but that fulfilment awaits you if you rediscover and pursue your true purpose for being here on earth.

Remaining aware of the bigger picture also helps when short-term sacrifices are required. It enables you to delay gratification of your immediate needs in order to fulfil your deeper spiritual needs. Sometimes your first glimpse of life's bigger picture can result in disappointment, especially when you realise how many of your pursuits are distractions from your true purpose here. When you experience the deep fulfilment which comes from the pursuit of a meaningful and spiritually rewarding life, those distracting pursuits you once treasured usually fall away from you.

CHAPTER TWENTY-SIX

Constructing a Map of Your Path

Now that you have examined how far you are into your life already and how long you feel you have left, the following exercise is designed to help you see when you've used excuses for not pursuing your goals or your purpose, and what you intend to do about it from now on.

Take a pen and paper, complete this exercise, and review it a week from now.

HABITS AND PATTERNS

- What have you done with your life so far?

- What excuses have you used to date for not pursuing your goals or your purpose?

- Whom have you blamed so far?

- Where are you right now in your life?

- List three important goals you are presently pursuing.

You are the common theme throughout your life, and you are free to take it where you want it to go — not necessarily immediately or without considerable effort, but free nonetheless.

Now it is time to look ahead to what you want from life. The following exercise is designed to help you focus on the *where* part of the equation.

WHERE ARE YOU GOING?

- Where do you want to be in your life one year from now?

- Where do you want to be two years from now?

- Five years from now?

- Ten years from now?

- How do intend getting there from here?

- Miracles aside, what steps can you take right now towards your goals?

From time to time, it is essential to ask yourself if what you are doing is leading you towards or away from your goals and your purpose in life. While our goals sometimes conflict with our purpose, at other times they coincide gracefully. Remembering that purpose is centred around what you give back to the world can help you to balance your goals with purpose.

We are led to believe that goals will fulfil us but, in fact, it is the other way around. After we meet our immediate needs, it is usually what we give back that feeds us spiritually. I am not referring to that feeling of warmth we experience when we donate money to charity or help out a friend in need. Rather, I am speaking of the long-term fulfilment that stems from contributing to life in our unique way. As mentioned previously, often what we give back is what we ourselves have struggled with. People who have been to the edge of the abyss emotionally can help others face their own darkness. Those who have overcome addictions can help others still in their grip. People who have had to master life alone and without the benefit of an experienced teacher can become that teacher for those on the same path.

If you have struggled to master financial discipline, you may be in a position to help others do the same, while those who have gone beyond loneliness can help others discover the joy of their own company. If still in doubt as to your purpose, look to the main issues in your life. Look to the main obstacles or hurdles you've had to leap, and you may glimpse what you can give back.

If you have yet to master those obstacles, begin now. People may help you along the path, while you'll also be in a position to assist others when you have faced your own issues.

The process is complicated, but the simplified version is set out below. How long you take with each step depends entirely on you and your circumstances. Resist the temptation to compare yourself with others, for we each have a different starting point in life. The process goes something like this:

- Identify one problem or issue.

- If that problem or issue were a puzzle, how might you solve it?

- What assistance will you require?

- How long do you expect to take?

- Identify the obstacles to solving your puzzle and how you'll deal with them.

- Proceed with the resolving of your issue, remembering that you already have all of the pieces of the puzzle and, if not, you can locate them in time.

- Contemplate what you might give back to the world when your life is more stable and rewarding.

Don't be afraid to seek assistance or support with any part of the journey or even the whole journey. At times we all must have our heroes, to encourage and inspire us, as we lick the wounds that result from rushing blindly into life.

Resist the temptation to compare yourself with others, for we each have a different starting point in life.

Having glimpsed life's bigger picture, you may realise that your life has no real direction. Once you rediscover your direction, you'll need a map to consult in order to stay on course. The best part about this map is that you have control over the direction you choose to take. The difficulty with this is that if you don't like the destination, you can't blame anyone but yourself.

You can add or remove people, situations, responsibilities and opportunities from this map at any point, according to your long-term needs. If your children move away from the family home and settle into their own homes with suitable partners, you might reassess the part they play in your map. Although they are still important to you, their day-to-day survival no longer depends on you, allowing you to focus more energy on your purpose.

CHAPTER TWENTY-SEVEN

Using Your Strengths in Career

Careers can be very rewarding, but only for those who find a career which suits them. You can spend many years eliminating those things that you don't want to do for a career, but there are always exceptions. I detest accountancy, but love numbers. A friend dislikes dealing with the public, but loves helping people. Benjamin is a natural therapist who loved to study, but hated the people aspect of his job. If he could have been paid to lecture or write articles on his chosen subjects, he'd have been a happy man. I sat opposite him in one consultation, and he peered clinically at me over his glasses as though thinking, 'So that's what humans look like'.

Because humans are a bundle of contradictions, we need to be careful not to eliminate possible aspects of general careers that we might find rewarding. Taking into account your need for variety or your tolerance for others, you may have to adjust your career choices accordingly. Ron likes variety, so his career comprises five different jobs in one. It involves regular interstate and overseas travel and teaching, which he loves. Ron didn't realise how much he enjoyed his career until he sat down to complete an exercise a friend gave him two years ago.

Louisa asked Ron to describe, in writing, what a perfect week would be for him. Although at first enthusiastic, he experienced a great deal of difficulty in completing the exercise.

It involves scripting a perfect week, from Sunday morning until Saturday night, without altering time to allow for things you aren't able to include in a real week. Ron finally finished it and, within six months, had experienced almost everything on the list. Perhaps he wasn't ambitious enough in drawing it up but, in reality, by crystallising what he wanted in his mind, he was preparing the way for such a week in reality.

Rather than ask you to do an exercise that might take three weeks, here is the simplified version. In simple terms, describe what a perfect working week would be for you. To make it easier, Ron's Monday is set out below:

- waking up in a hotel

- breakfast downstairs with potential CD distributor for Europe

- television appearance for new film project

- three radio interviews

- lunch with magazine editor and publicist

- meeting with actor and agent for next film project

- email distributors in Canada, Africa and Japan

- afternoon sleep

- opening night of current film, followed by brief meeting with marketing people

- dinner with partner

- late-night radio interview by phone

- swim in hotel pool

- sink into spa bath

- sleep

It is better to be precise about what you want, for if you leave something out, it is likely to be left out of your perfect week when it occurs. This exercise isn't about making it happen, but deciding what you'd like to have happen. Include the weekend even if you don't work at weekends, as you'll want to know how you rest and relax during your perfect week.

PERFECT WORKING WEEK EXERCISE

- List or describe your perfect working week.

- Include the type of work, the people you work with and the location.

- Feel free to mention your income for your perfect week.

- Describe the internal rewards you derive from your work.

- If you want to work only three or four days a week, mention that, also.

- Feel free to list a few things and then add to your perfect week over the next few days.

When clients complain that they don't know what career they are suited to, I ask them to do this exercise. Finding it hard to do is usually symbolic of their general life confusion. If you have difficulty with it, ask yourself: how can I move forward when I don't know which way I want to go?

I suspect that those who experience difficulties with this exercise are used to having others decide what is best for them. You need to decide for yourself in order to learn from experience.

If you decide on a perfect working week and then spend five years moving towards it, only to find that it doesn't fulfil you, there is only one person responsible: you. The good news is that if you progress towards a perfect working week and then decide that it's not as good as expected, you'll have developed the techniques to make things happen in your life. This means that scripting another perfect week and moving towards it will be easier.

Be honest with yourself. If you honestly think that you'll be happy working one day per week, then write that down. Unless you love your own company, be aware that boredom may set in if you have too much time on your hands while all your friends are at work.

When Ron listed a television interview and three radio interviews in his perfect Monday, he realised that he'd have to research and prepare those appearances. He'd have to read over his notes and examples from his film until he knew them backwards. With careful preparation and planning, he did make his examples appear natural and conversation-like. By compiling a list, Ron had become aware of the effort required beforehand.

A memorable talk Ron delivered was to a group of people in Boston. On a Wednesday talk series, he was the week's guest speaker. Many of those attending were regulars, a mixed bunch of around 45 people. As he glanced around the room at the end of question time, Ron realised that they had made him work hard, but that they were generous as an audience, on the whole. One woman at the back had sat chewing gum and knitting a jumper, and Ron figured she was there to keep him humble. Two men to one side had taken careful notes and asked difficult questions, quoting his words back to him in their questions. Ron had figured that they were there to keep him sharp. An elderly woman had asked him how old he was, and he had figured she was simply there to make him laugh. He had told her to save the flirting until the tea break.

After you've written up your perfect week, examine it carefully. Look at which aspects of it might make you dislike it. Review it a week from now and edit it, if required.

Having a point of focus helps with motivation and action. A great proportion of people who are chronically stuck in their lives. Seek out assistance in finding a purposeful career have many of the following characteristics in common:

- They are mildly depressed.

- They find it hard to discern opportunities, and usually see only the problems in a situation.

- They are not self-motivated.

- They haven't had a refreshing break or holiday in a long time.

- They often want others to push them into action and to take responsibility for them.

- They are afraid of making mistakes.

- They believe they've tried everything that might suit them.

- They are thinking in circles.

- They seek a standard job and don't look for a career that combines several things.

- Subconsciously they don't want to work to earn their living.

- They feel guilty about asking for what they consider is more than they deserve.

- They are emotionally immature, and feel cheated out of their childhood or adolescence.

- Sometimes they exhibit passive-aggressive tendencies, resisting any suggestions given them and failing to complete homework set for them.

- They want others to do all the work for them.

- They are often surprised when told that they are not serious about finding a suitable career.

- They have usually forgotten what they wanted to be in childhood.

- They don't actually believe that it is possible to change their lives and to enjoy a rewarding and well-paid career.

- They usually become more convinced when they have set small goals and achieved them through their own efforts.

- They 'know their place in life', but are torn between their belief that they ought to be happy with their lot and their desire to move on.

If you fit more than half of the above list, find someone to help you through the changes, lest you lose interest, become too tired to persevere or you sabotage yourself. Find someone independent of your life, someone objective. It's not always easy to find purpose, yet, without it, everything else is just marking time.

A friend recently commented on how much her partner Geoff had changed after he rediscovered his purpose. Note the term rediscover. Purpose is rarely lost, only forgotten or obscured by the demands of everyday life. She reminded me how lethargic Geoff used to be and how he constantly whinged about the jobs he had. He had always resented having to work for other people. It hadn't occurred to him at the time that he lacked the necessary discipline to make a success of life without the supervision of a boss.

Geoff dreamed of how free he'd be when he worked for himself and, since making the change, he has worked harder than ever. For two years he had worked as an employee for 30 hours each week and complained about the travelling time. Now he works in his own business and rarely puts in less than 60 hours a week.

Before you decide what it is you want to give back to the world, be sure you have the tenacity, strength and reserves of energy to do what you set out to do. Once you rediscover purpose, you'll have more motivation to work hard, but it will drain you from time to time. The difference is that you'll be almost driven to work hard, because you'll know that what you have to give is needed.

Purpose is rarely lost, only lost or obscured by the demands of everyday life.

Discovering what you can give back to the world means that you have to set some serious goals to realise that purpose. You may need to study, learn new skills, relocate or even learn another language. Setting these goals and reaching them is a part of your life. There's no hurry. You'll be giving back for as long as you live, so why rush it?

Another noteworthy point is that when you have rediscovered your purpose and are pursuing goals that will help you with it, a surprising number of people offer assistance. This support is usually enough to keep you on the path. Many clients start out with goals that are, in fact, a part of their purpose.

'If I can just get on top of my finances, I'll have a decent life,' said Leon, who mastered the lesson of financial discipline after a five-year struggle. He then applied his new-found discipline and purpose to other areas of his life.

'It's true, I hate myself,' stated Petra, staring at the floor. In learning to accept herself, she became more tolerant of others. Although it took almost four years, the work she did to improve her self-worth helped her towards a new career in social work.

It's no surprise that we are keen to apply what we have had to master within ourselves. Those difficult steps and the urge to give up and sink into depression, once overcome, strengthen us. It's not true that what doesn't kill you always makes you stronger. I've seen clients whose hopes have been crushed by the events of their lives. They weren't made stronger, but instead, watched as their strength, courage and hope ebbed away.

They grew strong again in various ways. Some restored themselves after they made sense of the events of their past. Others found hope in helping people. It's possible that a human chain is rarely as weak as its weakest link. This is because a human being can accept stress in many different ways. People can apply the stress to their strongest parts, and shoulder the burden longer. This was illustrated by June, who helped her friend, Anne, of 23 years through the breakdown of her marriage. Despite surviving a series of mild strokes and struggling with her own marriage, June encouraged Anne to pursue the life she dreamed of living. When Anne realised her goals, including leaving her husband and moving to the country, June was inspired to make her own goals a reality.

Generally speaking, frustration can be good, for it builds ambition — ambition to resolve the problems frustrating you, or ambition to make a new and different life. Sometimes life increases the pressure so that you sharpen your view and the perception of your opportunities, as happened with Frank, who collapsed at work one afternoon and was rushed to hospital. He had severe problems with his lower intestine and bowel that required a strict diet and regular exercise. He endured several operations and a great deal of physical pain, which sharpened his focus. More than anything Frank wanted to get well again.

Each time he broke his diet, he was admitted to hospital again. Soon he learned to be more disciplined. After fourteen months, he hardly ever missed what were once his favourite foods, including ice-cream, bananas, nuts and good red wine.

When Frank's health improved, he turned his new-found discipline to other areas of his life. Starting with his finances, he began saving money and then moved on to study. He took two courses he had been putting off and then applied the learning to make himself wealthy in real estate in the next ten years. Having no choice about his health taught Frank to see the stark reality of much of his life. He stopped procrastinating and decided that if he wanted to have a good life, he had to begin immediately.

Frank was confronted with the basic human purpose: to survive. Moreover, he has found his way to give back to the world, teaching street kids to discover their talents. Once a week he spends a day helping them learn to hope again. He offers them a chance for a better life, as he once hoped for that while lying in a hospital bed, alone. Frank admits that perhaps only one or two kids in every 25 he works with actually make a change in their lives. However, he is happy because he is purposeful.

Goal and purpose can coincide easily, especially when your goals further your progress towards your purpose. Whether it be studying for a certificate that will give you a job which is a part of your purpose or moving to another country where you can better fulfil your purpose, the achievement of each goal is rewarding both short and longer term. When your goals and your purpose conflict, it is evident because you can feel torn in two directions. One part of you wants the rewards which come from your goals while another part of you seeks a deeper peace and fulfilment which results from the pursuit of your true purpose. When this conflict occurs, you can achieve goals and still feel spiritually and emotionally hungry. The initial pursuit of purpose can leave you feeling unsettled, as you no longer pursue familiar goals. In this case, it is usually better to remember that purpose is ultimately what we are here for, whereas goals are only fleeting.

CHAPTER TWENTY-EIGHT

Where Purpose Cannot Be Found

Because purpose is not tangible, it cannot usually be found by looking at physical objects. It can, and is, often found when we stop looking and begin listening. When we listen for the part of us that remembers purpose, we find it.

Being born into a family can mean inheriting the family traits, sharing a family sense of purpose, perhaps even taking over a career or a project from your father or mother. Of course, this is not always the case, so by all means study your family traits and talents and decide for yourself whether your own purpose is contained with them.

Beware of those who are keen to tell you your purpose. Aside from the possibility of their having hidden agendas behind their assessment, the very process of self-discovery can be a part of the preparation for purpose. An example of being told your purpose by someone with an agenda comes from Janet, whose need for a purposeful path in life drew her to a guru. He told her that if she followed his path, he guaranteed that this would be her last lifetime and that she'd clear all of her past karma. Janet followed his directives, including surrendering all of her possessions and her savings to him, in the hope that she had, at last, found her true purpose. Four years later a deep spiritual longing resurfaced, and she realised that the guru's path was not her purpose after all.

Having no money and few friends outside the devotees of the guru, Janet faced the daunting task of embarking on a fresh search for her true purpose. It was made more difficult because she had allowed someone else to tell her what her life's purpose was, without questioning his motives.

School and university prepare people for careers, for fitting into life, but they rarely teach us how to find our purpose. So we probably attempt to do that by using the tools we might use to find a job or a new home. We look, search, scour, sort and examine possibilities, and perhaps become resigned to the fact that 'this must be it for me this lifetime'.

Purpose is rarely found in those things we have already accomplished, as these things often don't further our growth and development. Purpose isn't usually found in superficial experiences, but usually lies hidden. You'll know when you've found purpose, for you'll be filled with excitement, anticipation and dread at the possibilities. You'll hear your internal clock ticking and you'll probably want to start towards that purpose immediately.

This was the case with Collette, whose father bullied her throughout her childhood. As an adult Collette exhibited a very well-developed sense of fairness and justice, which drew her to becoming a union delegate for her workplace. She fought many battles, both at home and at work, and although at times exhausted, she always found the energy for another conflict or argument. Collette felt that she had found her purpose through fighting battles which life seemed to present to her constantly, whereas with careful observation this did not seem to be the case.

Beneath her struggling and continual conflict, Collette was preparing for the biggest hurdle she might face — confronting her father about his bullying. From an outsider's point of view, this was likely to be easy after the union battles she had already fought and won, but for Collette, it felt like an insurmountable hurdle. When she did finally conquer her fears and confront her father, Collette's need to fight union battles diminished and she was able to discover her true purpose. This involved working with teenagers, inspiring them to overcome their fears in order to pursue their dreams.

Having conquered her own greatest fear, Collette was an inspiration to hundreds of teenagers who were at risk of taking a path which would lead to conflict with the law and eventually with society. She is so comfortable and experienced with her life's purpose that some of the people she has helped are now bringing their teenage sons and daughters to her in the hope that she'll help and inspire them towards more rewarding lives.

Just for the record, purpose isn't found in a bottle, in demanding that life meet your needs unconditionally, or through sulking until the universe provides you with the life you desire. If you are doing any of these things then perhaps you're in life's waiting room. Perhaps you're waiting for your name to be called so that you can step out onto life's stage and be fabulous on the night without any training, experience or having squarely faced the setbacks which others have to face.

If you're in life's waiting room you are advised to make yourself very comfortable, as it is likely to be a very long wait indeed. Sometimes we need to fume, to sulk, or to resist life's attempts to move us forward, as frustration is often a positive thing. Frustration can build ambition; ambition to make up for the time you have spent waiting and to achieve what you know within yourself that you can achieve.

If you still want to sit in life's waiting room, take a good long look at the number on your ticket. It is probably as long as your telephone number, while the attendant has just called out, 'Number seven please'.

Purpose is not usually found in life's distractions. Some people become entirely engrossed in these and lose sight of their purpose. Distractions include the need for wealth, to be loved by someone in particular, to be famous, to be beautiful, to be admired, to be understood or to live life on your terms. In themselves these ambitions are okay, but if they distract you from your purpose you'll starve emotionally and spiritually until you feed yourself with what you've come into this life to do or to be.

Businesses are built and sold on their ability to meet the needs of people who are trying to become comfortable in life's waiting room. If you are settling in for the long wait, you might want your own personal waiting room, with cable television, air conditioning, deliveries from a local bakery and a wide variety of CDs to choose from. Waiting can become tedious, so distractions from the tedium are essential. None of these things are likely to further you in the pursuit of your purpose, but if you choose to go to sleep in your life, they make a wonderful accompaniment. In the end, even the most carefully planned waiting room is still a place to wait, and waiting isn't really living.

If you are in life's waiting room, you might want to ask yourself the following questions:

- Are you presently waiting in order to catch your breath after a challenging period?

- Are you waiting because you cannot face the path ahead?

- Are you waiting for life on your terms?

- Are you presently waiting because you cannot recall what you have come into this life to do?

- Have you been waiting so long that you have forgotten about your purpose entirely?

- Are you waiting for a sign from God or the universe that it is time to move forward again?

Waiting is necessary from time to time, especially if it allows us to reflect upon past goals and whether they helped or hindered us in the pursuit of purpose. Waiting for its own sake offers a half-life whose ultimate reward is likely to be regret. At the end of your life, will you regret those things which you have done, or those things you never dared to attempt?

CHAPTER TWENTY-NINE

Children: Little People with Big Purpose

Small children usually remember their purpose, but with all the information coming at them from every direction, it's not long before these memories fade. Although youngsters are often changeable, experiencing many different stages and interests, don't discourage them if they reveal an awareness of their purpose. Encouragement is the fertiliser of life. Great things can come from even a small amount of encouragement at the right time. Zola gives us an example of consistent encouragement. Her son Carlos loved to write stories when he was in primary school, and she encouraged the boy by reading every story he wrote. When he arrived home from school and she was tired, he'd still thrust an exercise book at her and insist that she read his latest effort. As she tells it, she had to wade through some of the most bloodthirsty literary outpourings she'd ever encountered, especially as Carlos entered adolescence.

Growing up, he learned that what he had to say through the written word was important, and that others were interested. He became a journalist and later an editor of a large-circulation magazine. His mother's encouragement had gone a long way to shaping his career choice. It is a part of his purpose.

The reverse occurred with Tiffany, whose father openly derided her whenever she attempted to do anything worthwhile. At eleven years of age, she applied for a job at the local grocery store, to be told by the owner that there were no vacancies at present, and that he'd call her if and when something came up. It was a case of 'Don't call us, we'll call you', politely presented to the young girl. When she told her father, he laughed at her, telling her that she'd been naive. Crushed, Tiffany decided not to allow herself to become excited by opportunities again. She grew cynical and bitter, and it took another 20 years before she was able to cast off the negative effects of her father's discouragement.

Just as it is essential to listen within for your own purpose, listening to your children may reveal their purpose to you.

During that time, even when life offered her real opportunities, she refused to become enthused. Even the thought of purpose at first seemed like a scam to her. She was hollow, but too fearful of being gullible to experiment with life.

Because the interests and tastes of children change as they grow and mature, it can be difficult to discern what this month's favourite is from what is a long-term possibility. Just as it is essential to listen within for your own purpose, listening to your children may reveal their purpose to you. Even the way a small child builds a mountain of blocks or draws a picture can reveal some of it. The important thing is not to encourage them in only one particular direction, but to simply observe what they are drawn to in life.

Children are offered more distractions today than at any other time in history. Toys, computer games, TV, video, DVD, the Internet, hand-held electronic games, musical instruments, board games, sports, mobile phones and email and keep them fully occupied. This leaves less time than ever for reflection and stillness. With a TV blaring in the background, and with a constant barrage of imagery and sounds coming at them, it's hard to be still. It's no wonder that attention deficit disorder (ADD) is on the rise amongst children.

With each passing generation, it is likely to become more and more difficult to find life purpose. There are so many things promising instant fulfilment. When children grow up believing that instantly gratified desires offer solutions to inner needs, why would they opt to make an effort that may not reward them for years?

Children who observe bees in flowers are watching them give back to nature, in order to have their needs met. In pollinating the flowers, the bees are giving something back. By bestowing on children whatever they want in order to keep them amused, we are not teaching them the value of giving something back to others. Instead, we are teaching that life will meet their needs endlessly.

It is time to encourage them is while they still recall their purpose, when they are still dreaming about the possibilities of a meaningful life. It is the time to nurture their purpose so that they can pursue it later in life, if they decide to do so.

CHAPTER THIRTY

When Purpose Eludes You

When a sense of true purpose eludes you, it is probably obscured by issues or problems you need to resolve. If you set about resolving them, you are likely to uncover your purpose eventually. Unresolved issues are not merely frustrations, they offer a chance to strengthen yourself before you are faced with the task of pursuing longer-term goals associated with your purpose. An example of this occurred with Johanna, who wanted to start her own business. She was a gentle, quiet and unassertive person, who had large debts that had to be repaid before she could begin saving for her business.

Although she had a goal (to begin a business) and a sense of purpose (to help others through counselling), she had to face the more practical concerns, her debts. In repaying them and controlling her spending, Johanna learned some valuable things about conscious spending. Her sense of purpose motivated her to complete her repayments rapidly and so she was in a position to open her business successfully.

In some cases, you are faced with problems but don't have the benefit of a sense of purpose to get you through your issues. In these instances, you need faith; you need to resolve your problems one by one, until your path is clear enough to glimpse your purpose. This was the case with Brett, who commenced counselling for relationship issues. Having resolved them seven months later, he realised that beneath those issues lay others waiting to be resolved. He continued counselling, resolving issues around low self-esteem, poor sleeping patterns, the need to be more assertive and to learn how to negotiate in order to have his needs met.

Brett described it as shovelling snow during a blizzard. As soon as he had cleared the path, it was covered again with fresh issues. Sometimes the hard work seems to be fruitless, until the path has been cleared. When this occurs, however, it is as though the resolution of one small issue has turned your whole life around.

What occurs is that the resolution of one final issue is enough to effect rapid change, after many other similar issues have already been resolved. You become more congruent physically, emotionally, mentally and spiritually; life becomes more fulfilling with less effort.

It can take months, years or even decades to reach this point, depending on from where you begin. It's the reward that is important. When you have cleared the path and you perceive your purpose, you'll be physically, emotionally and mentally fit enough to apply yourself to the task of pursuing that purpose. It's then that you'll realise how shovelling all that snow was, in fact, toning you up for the real effort.

After resolving the issues, look back over your past and decide what strengths you have gained as a result of your efforts. These strengths may be used in the pursuit of your purpose. Those who have no idea of their purpose and are overwhelmed by the issues demanding resolution might want help. Below are some possibilities:

AVENUES TO ASSIST YOU TO FIND PURPOSE

• Consult a careers adviser if you require a career purpose.

• Consult an experienced clairvoyant to ask about your life purpose.

- Consult a counsellor in order to clear the path for a glimpse of your purpose first-hand.

- Keep a dream diary, and examine your dreams for clues to your purpose.

- Meditate. Regular meditation to still your mind may allow your subconscious to tell you your purpose.

- Still your conscious mind with a walk along the beach or elsewhere in nature, and listen to your body.

- Remove yourself from the demands of everyday life by spending a weekend away or a few days in the country — in order to reflect and get a feeling of what is right for you.

Sometimes we need to remember what it's like to listen to our bodies, as we have spent years favouring the mind. When you are unaware of your physical body, the following exercise is often useful.

Jennifer and Chantal stand at opposite ends of a room facing one another. Jennifer becomes aware of how her physical body feels. While they maintain eye contact with one another, Chantal begins to walk towards Jennifer. It is up to Jennifer to stop Chantal's approach the moment she feels uncomfortable in her physical body with Chantal's proximity.

Chantal begins walking, slowly and deliberately, as they maintain eye contact. Subtle physical signs need to be observed, such as the breathing and the stance of each person. It is likely that Jennifer will tell Chantal to stop long after she has become uncomfortable. The telltale signs in Jennifer include holding her breath, swaying backwards slightly, as though to avoid a blow, bracing herself or perhaps blinking slowly and at length. It's the blink that says, 'I wish you weren't there'.

When asked to describe which part of her body told Jennifer she was uncomfortable with Chantal's proximity, she might name her stomach, or a tightened chest. The exercise is then repeated, with Jennifer being particularly aware of the part of her body she mentioned. Thus more alert to her body signs, she is able to stop Chantal the moment she feels uncomfortable, undoubtedly earlier in the process.

This exercise is designed to highlight how the physical body is a reliable barometer when you are uncertain which direction to pursue. Too often the mind is given to making important decisions while ignoring the reactions of the physical body. Apart from meditation, which may use the mind to decipher purpose, or dreams, which may reveal the contents of your subconscious mind, your physical body is more likely than anything else to guide you towards your purpose.

When purpose eludes you, it is possibly because you have eluded purpose, having learned to deftly avoid all the signals through which your purpose is conveyed to you.

Re-acquaintance with our physical body occurs for some of us only when it gives us trouble or collapses completely. When you are hospitalised, it's often too late to listen to your body, as it is often tranquillised by then. With its vital input suppressed, you are left with one less avenue of information about yourself and your reactions to the world.

When purpose eludes you, it is possibly because you have eluded purpose, having learned to deftly avoid all the signals through which your purpose is conveyed to you. If someone sends you a message and you refuse to acknowledge it, how will you know what they've been trying to tell you? It is as though you refuse to open any email with the heading 'Purpose'.

This is evident to all of us when we attempt to advise a friend who is putting up with a bad relationship. We tactfully suggest seeking help, leaving the relationship or approaching things differently, but the friend steadfastly ignores our advice. It is no different with your purpose. Parts of you are trying to convey your purpose to you at this very moment, but perhaps you cannot hear them due to the ingrained habit of ignoring your inner needs.

What prevents you hearing? All those unresolved issues and daily concerns that demand your whole attention. They take precedence over the purpose for your being alive this time around. Do you think that this is the way it ought to be? Does it seem right that you began with purpose and became lost in the desire to make the journey comfortable? Or maybe you were pushed off course and now cannot find a way back?

Enlisting the help of others can often mean finding that way back, in order to do what you came into this life to do. It's not easy to rebuild your awareness, especially if you didn't notice the incident or situation that took you away from your path in the first place.

Purpose lies within you, so it is essential to tune out all the outside noise and demands, in preparation for listening to the small voice within. That small voice cannot speak any louder, so it's best to have no distractions in order to hear it clearly.

In the course of an average day, how many things listed below distract you from listening to the small voice within? How many of them might be avoided for even 30 minutes a day or one hour a week, so that you can be re-acquainted with your intuition and your purpose?

- televison

- radio

- newspapers

- magazines

- the Internet

- your family

- drugs or alcohol

- work

- the telephone

- needy friends

- grief over past opportunities lost

- domestic responsibilities

You are the only one who can decide what really requires your attention. Perhaps your daily routines have clouded your purpose. It is possible that your life's purpose is much closer to you than you thought. Is it awaiting discovery beneath all the noise that is your crowded life?

Many people who attempt to meditate find it difficult, if not impossible, to sit still without their minds wandering. A guided meditation tape or CD may help. Having a friend or a teacher guide you through each step into meditation and bring you out again can help you let go and sink into a deep state of relaxation. If you don't have someone to guide you into meditation, find a meditation class or a simple course to help you to master the basics.

Strenuous exercise before meditation can also help. A client named Rosalie finds that a short run or ten minutes of stretching is the perfect preparation for meditation, as she thus reduces the muscle tension left over from the day. Don't expect miracles. Some people expect to listen to a guided meditation CD twice and have their purpose appear before them as a crystal-clear vision. It may take months.

USING MEDITATION TO DISCOVER YOUR PATH

- Meditate every day, stilling your mind of the internal chatter.

- Learn to ask yourself what you need to do next to clear the path to your purpose.

- Do what you found you need to do in step 2.

- Repeat steps 1, 2 and 3 until you achieve great periods of stillness in meditation. [For those who need additional help with meditation, I have designed a guided meditation CD offering four guided meditations. They range from a simple relaxation exercise to more advanced meditations. You'll find them on my website at www.academy-of-psychics.com.au]

- When you repeatedly achieve them, ask yourself about your purpose.

- If nothing springs clearly to mind, ask for guidance and be aware of yourself and your surroundings.

Purpose requires patience, both in locating it and in pursuing it. If you want an instant fix, the above method is probably not for you.

A more rapid method for illuminating purpose is one that can be more expensive. It involves asking someone else to help you: a counsellor or a life coach or a trusted friend. This person's role is to remind you when you stray from your path and to encourage you when you want to give up. On such a steep and winding path, there will be times when you'll find it too hard and you'll collapse, overwhelmed.

This is usually the time when you want to give up counselling, fire your coach or avoid your friend, but these are precisely the times when you most need support. Even if you have a counsellor or a friend to help you clear the path of all the debris your life has left there, you still have to do the work, to make the effort in order to reap the rewards.

A life coach is also useful when you are attempting to pursue career and other physical or mental goals that require attention to the path before you. Most of us are able to put a great deal of effort into a project for a short while. It's the long haul that saps our will or our concentration.

You can improve your chances of success by having someone in your life whose job it is to remind you about your goals and the search for your purpose. It could be a friend who has trodden the very path you are attempting to tread now. Having someone who believes in you and who is prepared to support you in a practical way is often priceless. Where the successful pursuit of goal or purpose is concerned, having someone standing beside you who believes in you can mean the difference between success and failure.

Connor was keen to improve his financial circumstances and provide an income for his retirement. At 34 years of age he had nothing to show for thirteen years of employment except a few clothes and a nice car, which he was still paying for. His friend Laslo owned two apartments in a block, which he rented out to tenants. Laslo became a role model for Connor, who grew excited at the possibility of owning an apartment, too. Despite his limited education and the fact that he'd emigrated to Australia only 20 years before with almost nothing, Laslo had worked hard to acquire real estate.

Connor took a second job and saved for three years. He rarely spent money on entertainment, luxuries or holidays, as Laslo kept reminding him of his goal to own an apartment. They discussed the possibility often and, when an apartment in the same building came up for sale, they looked at it carefully. Deciding that he did not have enough money to purchase the premises, Connor continued saving.

When a second apartment was offered for sale, Connor was ready. Together with Laslo, he viewed the apartment and arranged finance. He made an offer that was accepted after some negotiation. Now, six years later, Connor has recently purchased another apartment in a nearby building and is fulfilling his goal of a financially secure retirement.

During the first three years, as he saved the deposit, he felt overwhelmed several times. He wanted to give up, especially as he watched an apartment being sold to someone with much more money than he had saved. But Laslo encouraged him, reminding him how hard it had been for him fifteen years before when he had saved for his first apartment. Although Laslo wasn't coaching Connor on his whole life, he became a suitable role model and coach for one of the goals that Connor was pursuing.

If you can find suitable role models for each part of your life, this approach may work well for you. Or, if you prefer to have one person assist you in many different areas, then a counsellor or a life coach may suit you. One of the drawbacks to having a family member as a role model is that when you disagree on an issue unrelated to your goal, that person may no longer be effective for you. This was the case with Trent, whose sister Moira married a successful sailor named Gunther. Trent desperately wanted to learn to sail, and Gunther was happy to teach him. Trent, Gunther and friends spent many weekday afternoons and most Sundays on Gunther's boat out on the harbour. When Gunther put together a sailing team, Trent was included. Things went well until Gunther's marriage fell apart.

When Gunther divorced Moira, Trent was caught in the middle. Then Gunther commenced a new relationship and brought his new partner sailing. Meanwhile, Moira was suing him for child support. The situation soon became untenable and Trent had to find a new sailing team.

When your purpose eludes you, listen to yourself. Listen to those parts of which you may have been previously unaware, such as your feelings. Take time to be still by way of a walk amongst nature, meditation, an afternoon spent fishing or a few days in the country. In most cases you'll rediscover your purpose through being still enough to hear that small voice within. If not, seek out the assistance of an unbiased person in the discovery of your purpose. It is likely that purpose eludes you because for a long time you have eluded your purpose.

CHAPTER THIRTY-ONE

Seize the Day

It's an easy way out of having to find and pursue your purpose to say, 'I'm too old now'. For two extreme examples of proof that you're never too old and that you're already too old, we need only look at Marjorie and Alison.

Marjorie felt that her purpose was to be loved and she was actively seeking her next love relationship. At 96 years of age, she was leaving nothing to chance, enhancing her prospects somewhat by lowering her age to 91 when in mixed company. Marjorie cast an appraising eye over any potential suitors, planning on leaving behind a list of broken-hearted men when she departed this earth.

Alison, on the other hand, openly stated that 'I'm too old to learn new things or to change now. I'm 26 years old, for God's sake!' In contrast to Marjorie, she had managed to grow old with exemplary speed and determination ...

One thing they had in common was that they didn't usually mix with people their own age. Marjorie mixed 'with the sixties set', while Alison mixed predominantly with serious people in their late forties.

Their beliefs about life were illustrated clearly by their comments. With a cackle of a laugh, Marjorie declared, 'If God didn't want us to drink, he wouldn't have given us thirst', whereas Alison stated, 'I don't let loose very often because I have so many responsibilities'.

It's rarely too late to discard some of your responsibilities in favour of your true purpose. Cemeteries are filled with people who believed that the world was going to stop the moment they died, because no-one was likely to assume all their responsibilities.

If it is your purpose to accept responsibility for the workings of your company, town, city or country, then give it your best shot. If, however, your responsibilities are detracting from your purpose, perhaps it is time to find a way to ease back on the responsibilities in favour of purpose. Even on your deathbed, it is possible to realise your purpose. It may be too late to pursue and accomplish it at that point, but it is rarely too late to recognise it.

Stop making excuses, seeking elaborate justifications or blaming others for where you are presently. Look for the reason you are here in the first place. You have something to contribute, something to give to the rest of humanity and, large or small, we need it.

Perhaps you're a late starter. Alternatively, you may have become aware of your purpose early. An example of this occurred last year. Due to a sudden cold snap in early summer, my 65 sunflowers bloomed early. Thinking that winter was approaching, they fulfilled their purpose of producing seeds to ensure another crop next summer. We rarely know how long we have left and whether the time we have is measured in years or in weeks. This makes the pursuit of purpose in the short term is essential.

Anthea awakened to her purpose at the age of 49. Having worked as a nurse since she was seventeen, she decided to prove to herself that she was capable of further study. She enrolled at university and graduated four years later. Empowered by her success, Anthea completed several personal interest courses, travelled around the world and pursued a new career.

Throughout her life Anthea had wanted to be an artist, but had felt inadequate, lacking confidence in her ability. After completing her degree, she took painting classes and private lessons with a successful painter whose style she admired.

By the age of 60, Anthea was exhibiting her paintings in various galleries and earning a steady income from doing something she loved to do. She had pursued her purpose and was supporting herself by what she was giving back to the world.

Caroline, a plump but spritely woman in her late sixties, had spent most of her life teaching. For the past ten years she had been teaching prenatal classes and relaxation exercises. Now she felt jaded with her workload and consulted me for a clairvoyant reading.

You have something to contribute, something to give to the rest of humanity and, large or small, we need it.

Her questions centred around career, but it was actually clarity of purpose she was seeking. As a teacher, she was looking for new ways to reach the public. It soon became apparent that she'd be involved with creating videos and DVD discs for sale to the public. She confirmed that she was indeed about to undertake a video film-making course. With renewed purpose, Caroline set off to climb the next career mountain. Her purpose was still to teach, only through a different medium.

Using the excuse that it's too late to do or to learn what you've come to learn this lifetime may still your conscious mind, but it won't quiet your spirit. One of the symptoms of not pursuing your purpose in life is a tension between the fulfilment of your outer (or conscious) goals and your inner (or spiritual) needs. Sometimes we see fabulously successful people who are completely miserable because they are not fulfilling their spiritual purpose in life. It doesn't have to be a choice between the outer and inner needs. Sometimes you can meet them both through choosing the right path for you this lifetime. If there is conflict, however, the dissipation of tension between the outer and inner needs often requires that you meet the inner needs first.

CHAPTER THIRTY-TWO

A Metaphor for Purpose

I've been teaching classes since 1985 and occasionally I meet a former student and we chat for a few minutes. In many cases they have not kept up their studies but it's often surprising how many of them recall the stories I used to illustrate each point during their lessons.

People like stories as they offer a simple way to absorb a lesson or a point without all the technicalities. In many cases, a good story brings data to life.

Nicholas ran his fingers through his thinning grey hair while sitting indoors at a café table, devouring lunch near a window overlooking the bay. David glanced around, his youthful curiosity unmasked. Seagulls perched on all available surfaces, and one cheeky bird stood on the window ledge, staring in at the diners. A pair of experienced sailors, the men were discussing life's journey, particularly their careers, using a boat as a metaphor.

'We've been looking at life's journey through the eyes of those who sail alone in a small boat. But what about those who choose to spend their lives on larger boats?' queried Nicholas.

'Such as?' asked David.

'Such as the SS *Corporation*,'* Nicholas replied, with a twinkle in his eyes, and David nodded.

'When you put it that way, I see a frigate or a destroyer, crowded with weapons, goods for sale and staff scurrying to and fro.'

'When you consider how many of us choose to sail through life protected by a corporation, it makes sense to also look at other forms of sea transport.'

'The SS *Corporation* is not for me,' stated David flatly.

'Perhaps not, but for many people, this is a suitable and comfortable form of transport. You are unlikely to be tossed around in poor weather in a frigate, compared to a small boat like yours.'

'That's true, but unless you're the captain, it might be a hard voyage. Think about all those people who work below deck, rarely seeing the sun and breathing fresh air.'

'How much sun and fresh air did you see during your last storm?' countered Nicholas.

'You give up life and death in smaller storms in favour of safety and stability, but it costs you some great views and sunsets.'

'Something like that,' replied Nicholas. He continued. 'How about life aboard the SS *Cruiser*? It sails through tropical islands on a monthly basis, offering both stability and entertainment. It also offers interesting localities and tennis, swimming, movies, several bars and nightclubs and the possibility of romance almost every night of the week.'

'It sounds tempting, as long as you are a guest and not a staff member,' replied David.

'Are you suggesting that for the staff it's all work and no play? Don't you think they fraternise with the guests, despite constant reminders not to do so from the management?'

'When you look at it that way, the SS *Cruiser* looks much better than the SS *Corporation*,' Nicholas went on. 'I guess that the difference might be that when you alight the SS *Corporation*, you may have enough funds to purchase your own boat, whereas those alighting the SS *Cruiser* often have more memories than savings.

'Now, on a smaller scale, the SS *Summer Fun* is a charter boat for snorkelling around local beaches, islands and coral reefs. It is a large, high-powered catamaran, which spends the days at sea and the nights in port.'

'That's my kind of boat! Days at sea in the sun and nights at home by the fire or in a warm dry bed suit me perfectly.'

'It has its drawbacks, too.'

'Like what?' asked David as he reached for another crusty roll.

'Well, the winter months. There are few tourists then, so you may need to earn enough through summer to get you through a third of the year when you have little or no income.'

'That doesn't sound too bad, really,' David commented.

'Then how about a tropical storm scaring away tourists, or competition setting up close by and offering cheaper, shorter cruises for those who only want to be out on the water long enough to take a few photos and tell their friends that they sailed?'

'Yes, but you'd have competition aboard the SS *Corporation*, too.'

'True,' answered Nicholas, 'but you wouldn't necessarily feel it directly.'

'Until changing its name to the SS *Redundancy*,' replied David, laughing as he sipped his chilled white wine. 'It might be downsized, right-sized or even capsized if it fell into the hands of bad management.'

'But chances are you'd still walk away with a financial package and the knowledge that many others were in the same situation,' reasoned Nicholas.

'That's no consolation.'

'Until you realise that the SS *Corporation* has lifeboats. Does the SS *Cruiser* have readily deployable lifeboats?'

'A good point,' David conceded. 'So what other options are there?'

'Well, there's the SS *Just-a-few-of-us*,' said Nicholas.

'What's that like?'

'It's a mid-sized cabin cruiser that sleeps twelve at a pinch, but is better suited to cocktail parties, weekends away and a business syndicate involving up to ten people. They might invest in real estate or have shares in a restaurant or a mid-sized business, and they sail away at weekends.'

'Sounds fine. Where do I sign?' quipped David.

'It, also, has its drawbacks.'

'Such as?'

'Well, even if you fall out with anyone in the syndicate, you are still under obligation to sail at the weekends.'

'It's starting to sound like a sentence now,' remarked David.

'Yes, it can be. Imagine how you might feel, having to sail all weekend beside someone who has just lost you a fortune due to poor management or a series of bad decisions. You might want to throw him overboard, but you are obliged to be civil.'

'It's really beginning to sound a lot like the SS *Corporation*.'

'Well yes,' agreed Nicholas, 'it has its element of politics, but on a smaller, more intimate scale. At least on the SS *Corporation*, you can transfer to another department or even another vessel, being another branch of the company. Aboard the SS *Just-a-few-of-us*, you have only one vessel, which often travels the same route each weekend.'

'Okay, so what else is there?'

'There's the SS *Sole Trader*,' replied Nicholas. 'A smaller vessel, sleeping up to four at a time. It is more prone to damage or even to breaking up in a bad storm, but it is also much more agile and manoeuvrable than the previous vessels.'

'So what are the drawbacks?'

Nicholas chewed on some bread for a few moments before he spoke. 'Well, there are some, as expected. If you are ill, you cannot sail. If you are ill for too long, your vessel may be repossessed by the bank or by your creditors. The SS *Sole Trader* is susceptible to leaks and requires constant maintenance or it may sink. I've heard it said that 95 per cent of all vessels named SS *Sole Trader* sink within ten years of construction.'

'Ninety-five per cent of them! That's outrageous,' exclaimed David, with a full mouth. 'And what happens to the other five per cent?'

'Some of them become an SS *Just-a-few-of-us*, some may even be converted into an SS *Summer Fun* and, very rarely, one may be the basis for an SS *Corporation*. It's rare, but it has been known to happen.'

'The SS *Sole Trader* is looking like a decidedly risky boat to sail in,' David concluded.

'It's not all bad. You might recall some glorious sunsets seen from the deck of your boat, and the joy of entering a new harbour or leaving one that you didn't enjoy.'

'Yes, all that and more.'

'So why don't you sell me on the benefits of the SS *Sole Trader*, since you're sailing in one?' said Nicholas, as the waiter removed his plate.

'The benefits of the SS *Sole Trader* include sailing whenever you want, for as long or short a period as suits you. You can change direction without having to consult superiors, and you can travel with company or alone. You choose the direction and the distance you want to cover each week and if you decide to quit sailing, you simply sell your boat.'

'It sounds almost too good to be true,' was Nicholas's response as he looked up at a waiter offering him a dessert menu.

'Well, yes, but the gloss wears off when you are plugging a leak, have lost your map and are suffering with seasickness due to a tropical storm. Your back aches, your fingers are numb with the cold as you make your fifth attempt to tie a rope, while another wave washes over you. When you're not risking being washed off deck, you are praying to the god of the sea, Poseidon, that an enormous wave doesn't snap your boat in two and suck you under.'

They ordered dessert, and a waiter folded back the windows, allowing the breeze to engulf them. The cries of the gulls forced them to speak up to be heard.

'So which do you think is the best vessel?' asked David.

'The best vessel for me isn't necessarily the best vessel for everyone,' responded Nicholas.

'Yes, I realise that, but which one do you like the best?'

'I'm with you. I like the SS *Sole Trader*, because when you have found a tranquil passage to frequent, it is a pleasant sailing experience indeed.'

'But who would want the other boats?'

'Well, Rick, a friend of mine, for one,' replied Nicholas. 'He'd like the SS *Corporation* until he had saved enough to build the SS *Just-a-few-of-us*.

'I guess it depends on your sailing abilities, your needs and the lifestyle you want for yourself long term.'

'I can't imagine enjoying any of the other types,' mused David. 'That may be so, but I know of a man who started sailing in the SS *Sole Trader* and one day woke up to discover that he had moved on to sail an SS *Just-a-few-of-us* — before finally becoming the big man on the bridge of the SS *Corporation*. I met him staring enviously at me as I ambled off to work on my boat. My life was a reflection of his youth, and for a moment, he wanted it back again. I'm sure that had I wanted to, I could have sold him my boat on the spot for a handsome profit.'

CHAPTER THIRTY-THREE

An Illustration of Purpose

'So what do you think is the difference between a goal and purpose?' asked David over coffee. Toying with a square of dark chocolate, Nicholas pondered the question.

'Let's consider that waiter,' started Nicholas. 'He is proficient at his work. He's been effective in managing the room and discreet in taking orders, delivering the food and removing plates. What do you think his purpose might be?'

'To help the customers?'

'No, that's a goal.'

'To increase his tips,' continued David, with a grin.

'That's another goal.'

Nicholas took a bite of his square of chocolate. Shards of the rich sweet melted on his warm tongue before he replied. 'If he desired to become an excellent waiter, we might say he had a purpose. If he desired to have the dining room cleared and the tables set by 4 pm, we might agree that he had a goal. Perhaps the difference here is that even when he realises his purpose, his journey has just begun. When he reaches his goal, it has been achieved and is likely to be replaced by another. Being an exceptional waiter is a purpose that can be experienced for years at a time.'

'So are you saying that a purpose takes longer to achieve than a goal?'

'Not quite. I think that purpose is about being, whereas goals are about doing. When one acts with purpose, one is aware of the consequences of actions.'

David's next question came at once. 'So how does purpose differ from a goal?'

'The two words are often used to mean the same thing, but where life purpose is concerned, you cannot substitute goals for purpose. How often have you heard people use the term life goal?'

'Let me get this right. You mentioned that when you realise a goal, a new need surfaces?'

'Yes,' replied Nicholas. 'Goals are often destinations. Purpose is the journey.'

Purpose is about being, whereas goals are about doing.

'You seem to be saying that when you realise your purpose, you need to refine it?'

'Yes, that's about it.'

'Refining your purpose might take as long as realising it in the first place,' David said.

'That's right, but where's the race?' asked Nicholas, savouring the chocolate.

'Do you think that goals are less important than having or realising purpose?'

'No, both are important. It's just that having a list of goals without a long-term purpose can make the achieving of the goals a hollow victory.'

Nicholas continued. 'When you embark on the path towards another goal, it might be wise to ask yourself if it will enhance or detract from your purpose.'

'That is, of course, provided you know what your life purpose is in the first place,' muttered David. 'What happens when you fall ill, for instance? Surely your goal then is to regain your health. In that case, your immediate goal must supersede your purpose?'

'Not really,' answered Nicholas. 'Your goal is perhaps to have good health again, and your purpose is what makes returning to good health worthwhile. If you were seriously ill, it might pay you to ask the following question: what will I do with my life and good health if and when it returns? To what purpose will I devote my good health?'

The waiter approached and topped up their coffee cups before removing the dessert plates. His swift, adept movements revealed years of experience. The simple act of removing plates from a table was almost a scene from a ballet, which he could have performed with his eyes closed.

'So what is your purpose?' asked David suddenly.

'I'm a teacher,' replied Nicholas. 'I'm one who assists others in their search.'

'So how did you discover that?'

'It is something I have always done. As a child I was the teacher of my younger siblings, because my parents were very busy. Perhaps it was a compensation for my not having instructive, far-seeing parents. Some days I wonder if I've taken on my childhood role and made it my purpose. It's possible that my childhood was actually a training time for my purpose,' he said, staring out to sea.

'You seem to be a natural teacher. So whether you have grasped something you did well in your childhood and made it your purpose, or your childhood was actually training, for your purpose, the result is the same. You still have a sense of purpose.'

'Yes, I do.'

Silence ensued. Nicholas recalled the doubts he had experienced as a teacher accepting that he was in a position to assist others towards their purpose. He still occasionally felt like an impostor, especially when his purpose became obscured by immediate issues.

He realised that Nicholas was sharpening his perceptions. It was as though asking the right question here might make the difference between finding his life purpose now or much later in life. Leaning forward, he asked eagerly, 'Do you always know the way for yourself?'

'No, I don't. I need other guides from time to time, people to point the way as well as guidance from within. I find this during periods of reflection in the garden.'

Stirring his coffee, David pondered this.

'I've realised my purpose, now I'm refining it. Refining purpose is a long-term process.'

'Teaching others wouldn't be enough for me,' observed David.

'Don't measure your purpose by how many people it will affect directly. When you find your purpose, it affects each of us in a subtle way. As I understand it, with every person who finds their path, we all have more love and light to go around. Conversely, for everyone who remains in the dark, we all share their burden, their confusion. The way I see it, every person who is pointed in the right direction we all benefit from.'

Nicholas sipped his coffee and continued. 'I look around and notice many people who have forgotten what it feels like to act with purpose. Some of them cannot recall what it means to be alive with a sense of purpose. They experience a sense of emptiness. Take our waiter friend. If he had no purpose, what is the point of being good at his job? What is the point of increasing his knowledge of food and wines, his skills in the kitchen and out here on the floor, and his knowledge of the needs of regular customers? None whatsoever. He might as well be doing just any job, for it is unlikely to lead towards purpose or increase a sense of purpose.'

'Can't jobs be done simply to earn enough money to be able to do something else?'

'Yes,' sighed Nicholas. 'They can, but since our jobs take up much of our waking lives, they might as well be purposeful, don't you think?'

'Sure. Suppose our waiter was working in this restaurant to earn enough money to become a singer or to study natural therapies or even to get his brother out of a foreign jail. That means that he might not be interested in learning all about food and wines, as his job was basically a means to an end.'

'It's quite possible, but if you look at the bigger picture, you may notice something. Let's say, for argument's sake, that he is saving to get his brother out of a foreign jail, and that next week he'll be flying off to collect his long-lost brother. After sixteen months of waiting on tables, our friend has achieved his goal of setting his brother free. Now what happens after his brother is released? Doesn't another goal surface? Perhaps he has to resettle his brother ... And after that, another goal.'

'Then what would you call it,' asked David, 'if he went back to waiting on tables in order to rescue many people from jails in foreign countries?'

'I'd say that you might be seeing a goal being reshaped into a purpose.'

'He is still not keen to improve his skills as a waiter, because he doesn't see waiting on tables as his purpose,' said David triumphantly.

'True, but if his goal is to raise as much money as quickly as possible to release people from prison, then increasing his skills and knowledge as a waiter might improve his tips. He might also find a position in an exclusive restaurant where his gratuities are five to ten times greater than in his present position. So. actually, his job is an important part of his purpose. Goals and purpose can be integrated.

'So what goal have you combined with your purpose?' asked David.

'Study. As a teacher, I continually increase my knowledge of life to have as many possibilities as I can to offer my students. Study, travel, courses, new friendships and experiences all feed my purpose.'

With every person who finds their path, we all have more love and light to go around.

David pondered this as they left the café and made their way into town again. The turbulent grey sea drowned out the seagulls further along the empty beach as they turned towards the town square.

'Goals are the steps towards and within purpose. Goals can lead to purpose or be simply for their own sake. Purpose makes the goals worthwhile.'

'Do you mean that the more of your life map you are, the easier it is to weather the storms in life?' asked David.

'Yes, purpose lends strength and courage in the pursuit of your goals.'

CHAPTER THIRTY-FOUR

Different Perceptions of Purpose

The following day Nicholas saw David sitting alone and wandered over to say hello. David was startled as he was deep in thought and didn't see his friend approach.

'How many possible purposes are there to choose from?' he asked. Nicholas smiled as he sat down beside him. Two seagulls fought over a fish head that had been tossed from a boat onto the golden sand. Their screeching and squawking attracted more gulls. Their cries reached a crescendo, until a dog appeared and drove them all away, collecting the meal for herself.

Nicholas replied. 'I've heard that in ancient Greece there was a school of thought that suggested only five basic purposes in life. There were subgroups to these five purposes, naturally, but any purpose you cared to name came under one of the five headings.'

'What were these headings?' asked David attentively.

'They may seem unlikely at first, but they are only headings. This allows for new careers and discoveries in life, while these headings remain current throughout the centuries.'

'Yes, what are they?' interrupted David.

'They are **doing, conserving, experimenting, understanding and remembering.**'

'What? They don't sound the least bit like purposes to me,' said David, completely disheartened. He was suddenly tired of riddles and wanted some direct answers to pressing questions about the purpose of it all.

'Allow me to illustrate each heading and perhaps you'll agree that all purposes fall under one of these headings.'

'Fire away.'

'The first is **doing.** Those whose purpose is to do, the doers, are physically active. They build houses, start businesses, enter competitions, run marathons and achieve in sports. They push the accepted boundaries, venturing forth where ordinary men and women don't dare to tread. They explore new territories, invent new machines and technologies, and generally tire out all those who observe them for any length of time. Do you know anyone like this?'

'Yes. I have a sister who is a doer. She can't sit still, and she has unbelievable reserves of physical stamina.'

'So I guess she probably doesn't have a lot of patience with those who can't keep up?'

'You bet. She thrives on a challenge and responds well to being dared to attempt something new,' David replied, smiling.

'The second group are the **conservationists,**' continued Nicholas. 'These people are keen to preserve the way things have always been done, and they resist any attempt at innovation suggested by the doers. They are solid, reliable types, who are trusted in an emergency. In a way, they keep their communities ticking along smoothly. They dream of trains running on time, and they prefer reliability to innovation. Do you know anyone like that?'

'Half my family are like that. Both of my parents are conservative. They are always cautioning me against taking risks and trying new things. These are people who prefer to holiday in the same place year after year.'

'They sound like conservers.'

'What about the next type?' David was intrigued.

'These are the **experimenters**. They are innovative, become bored easily and love to try new things. Any new fad or trend is quickly adopted by them. They are the reason fashions change so often. They are why restaurants alter their menus from season to season. These people love new experiences, new acquaintances, new horizons and anything different. Taking a holiday to the same place each year is hell to them. Do you know anyone like that?'

'My previous partner, Lucy. She was an impulsive woman and full of optimism. She changed her mind as quickly as she changed her hair colour or her clothes. Her friends were from all walks of life, and the list of jobs on her resumé didn't look possible for one person. Lucy left in the end because she grew tired of me.'

'She sounds like an experimenter.'

'So what is the next type?' David asked.

'These are the **understanders**. Those whose purpose is to make sense of life. Those who long to understand themselves, others and life itself. These people study humanity, through philosophy, psychology, comparative religions and foreign cultures. They are

Those whose purpose is to do, the doers, are physically active.

unambitious unlike the doers, they are not usually found at sporting events or competitions where physical ability leads to success. The understanders are the people to consult when life isn't making sense. They have a way of helping people to fathom causes of events and they can remind them of the bigger picture. Do you know anyone like that?'

'You seem like that to me,' replied David.

Nicholas smiled.

'You said that there were five types. What is the fifth?' asked David.

'The fifth type is less common in the Western world. They are the **rememberers**. They remember not the petty details of what happened last week, but the bigger picture. They remember that we are spiritual beings in physical bodies. As a consequence, they are less involved in the material world.

'They are suited to religious or spiritual life, and they make excellent reminders of our long-term spiritual journey. They usually avoid competition. They are not flighty and do not seek out new experiences like the experimenters. They have no interest in ensuring that practical concerns run smoothly as do the preservers, and they are close in viewpoint to the understanders. Whereas the understanders are aware of the need to earn a living and that philosophy is only a part of life, the rememberers live with the knowledge that their physical bodies don't belong to them. They believe that ultimately, attending to spiritual purpose is vitally important. Do you know anyone from this group?'

'Not currently. I had a friend who was a painter, around ten years ago. She was as you described. Dreamy, other-worldly and more interested in the spirit than in the body.'

'From your description, she is probably a rememberer.'

'Are all possible purposes found under these headings?'

'Yes, according to the ancient Greeks. I've also been working on another list of headings.'

'Oh? And what are they?'

'Well, they are a work in progress,' replied Nicholas, 'but I feel they will prove to be accurate eventually.'

'What are they?' asked David, impatiently.

'They include **teaching, loving, healing, goading and understanding.**'

'Can you give me examples?' asked David.

'Sure. The **teachers** enjoy learning and helping people to learn and make use of their new-found knowledge. Whether it be teaching in a classroom or training the new person in the office, teachers help.

'**Lovers** spend their lives loving others. Whether they focus all their love on one person, or love their family, friends and neighbours, these people heal themselves and others through the act of continuously loving. Some people find them too naive and trusting, and not discerning enough as to who deserves their love, but the lovers feel incomplete until they are loving someone.'

'The next type are the **healers**. Healers cover many avenues, including medicine, dietary healing, natural therapies, psychology, psychiatry, research chemistry, and so on. These people have an innate urge to improve the lot of others. They thrive where they can help others who are falling behind, whether through ill-health or emotional stress. We need the healers in all their varieties, from the traditional shamans to surgeons.

The goaders

force us to find

a new approach

to a problem or

an ongoing

situation.

'The next type are the **goaders**. Although they frustrate everyone around them by goading them into action, they are useful indeed. The goaders force us to find a new approach to a problem or an ongoing situation. They can be stubborn, determined and even sometimes downright obnoxious. Their purpose is to frustrate and annoy us in order to sharpen our perception and to shock us out of complacency. There is usually one goader in every large office, on every football team and in every extended family. They often excel in times of war; they sometimes exhibit great courage. They relish the challenge of a battle.

'The last type are similar to the ancient Grecian understanders. These people perceive life as a puzzle. They embrace philosophy and spirituality, and they enjoy studying of human nature.

'Do you know people of all these types?' he asked David.

'Yes. Yes, I do. Even the goaders, which is a strange category.'

'They are, but they serve a useful purpose.'

'As if life didn't have enough frustrations, without adding a goader to the mix?'

David spent the following days scrutinising those around him to decide in which category they belonged. After testing the theory of the five basic types held by the ancient Greeks, he wanted to know more.

He badgered Nicholas for more information. Nicholas invited David to search through the books in his library. David leapt at the offer but was stopped in his tracks when he discovered that Nicholas's private library was almost as large as the local community library.

Fifteen months later, David read books from his friend's library, one of the most recent being a book on the ancient study of cheirology, or palmistry. A thick, yellow-paged book offered David an insight into the five types, despite its tattered cover and loose binding. The word cheirology is related to the ancient Greek-derived prefix chiro (kiro), meaning hand. David has discovered five distinct shapes of hand, which correspond to the five basic approaches to life. His search continues.

CHAPTER THIRTY-FIVE

Trusting Your Instincts

Your body is a barometer and in listening to it and to your instincts, you can avoid trouble and improve your life. It also serves as a compass if you are prepared to take the time to recognise its signals.

Sandra is a good example of trusting her instincts. She was trying to sell her house and, after several months of limited interest from buyers, she felt depressed. A couple viewed the property one afternoon and seemed interested. They came back a second time and made a verbal offer, which Sandra felt was too low.

The couple viewed her home a third time and told her that they'd send a written offer the following Friday. Friday came and went without an offer, and Sandra became impatient. She stated aloud that if the couple had not made a written offer by Tuesday afternoon, she'd forget about them and continue her efforts to get other offers. Later she explained she had an instinctual feeling that she was going to sell the property for $8000 more than the present offer.

On Wednesday morning the agent called Sandra, saying the couple wanted another viewing of the house. Sandra told him she was not interested. Their attitude changed upon hearing this. They produced a written offer immediately, which Sandra declined, to their surprise. The agent urged her to accept it as there were no other interested parties, but she held firm. The next day, Thursday, another couple viewed the property and, on Friday, they made an offer that was $8000 higher than the previous one. Sandra's instinct proved correct.

Sometimes, despite clear information about what we are better off avoiding, we ignore our instincts and proceed regardless. When Amber arrived for a palm reading, she was unable to place her hands flat on the table due to a serious car accident. It turned out that, seven years previously, she and her partner, John, both addicted to heroin, had argued fiercely one afternoon. They decided to separate. John had wanted to venture out into a storm to purchase more heroin, but Amber wanted to remain at home. Though John had urged her to accompany him, she felt uneasy about the trip.

Your body is a barometer and in listening to it and to your instincts, you can avoid trouble and improve your life.

Ignoring her instincts, however, she had set off with him. John fell asleep while driving, and the head-on collision killed him and the driver of the car he hit. Amber had been laid up in hospital for nearly nine months with a broken neck, arms, leg and ribs. Doctors told her that she was lucky to be alive, and to expect her spinal vertebrae to disintegrate as she aged, as a result of the accident. It was almost an annihilating experience for Amber, who recognised afterwards that she had known within herself that her actions that day were unwise.

In some cases, instinctual information is available, and we ignore it repeatedly until it can no longer be overlooked. Sara fell in love with a married man. William had no intention of leaving his wife and children, yet Sara lived in the hope that they might one day be together as a couple. After six years, she ended the affair. Two years later, William divorced his wife when the last child left home. He phoned Sara from the nearby railway station saying, 'I'm at the station with a bottle of champagne. I want to see you'.

The affair resumed, but did not deepen, as William offered Sara no more commitment than previously. She ended it twelve months later, collapsing into depression as a result of living in hope for so long. Six months later, William phoned out of the blue to say that he was nearby and wanted to see her. Sara ignored her instincts again and allowed William to visit her. The pattern was repeated.

Five months later, Sara ended it again, saying she should have listened to her instincts in the first place. She felt that William had cost her almost eight years of her life. Seven months later, William phoned Sara again to say, 'I have a bottle of champagne, I'm at the station and I need to see you'. Sara replied, 'Get on the next train and drink the champagne on your way home. Goodbye.' She felt relieved as soon as she ended the call. She has not heard from William since.

Perhaps Sara had a spiritual lesson to learn from her years spent trying to be in a love relationship with William. It is also likely that she may have spared herself a great deal of pain by trusting her instincts in the first place.

For some of us, the idea of a new opportunity is appealing. We don't stop to ask ourselves if we actually want what is being offered. For the enthusiastic types, the following questions might help. When being presented with an offer or an opportunity, ask yourself:

- Do I want this?

- What will I have to give up or forgo in order to have this?

- What will achieving this cost me physically, financially, emotionally, mentally or spiritually?

- Do I have room in my life for this at present?

- Once I have realised my goal, what will it cost me to maintain it?

- Are there better opportunities ahead if I forego this one?

- How long, realistically, will it take me to realise this goal?

- How many of my previous goals took more out of me than I imagined at first?

- When I think about this goal, how does my body feel? (Look beyond anticipation and excitement. Look for fear, dread, tension or an unnatural urgency.)

- Do all the parts of me feel right about this? Physical body, emotions, mentality? And instinct?

When you feel right about a project or a direction, pursue it wholeheartedly.

CHAPTER THIRTY-SIX

In Pursuit of Your Purpose

There is no magic formula or set of steps that, when taken in the correct order, will open your eyes to your life's purpose. While some of us cannot seem to find our purpose, others cannot forget it.

Gavin sometimes tried to forget his purpose so that he might live a peaceful life. Peace is illusive for those who know their purpose but do not follow it. Trying to hide from his purpose, Gavin immediately felt as though he was drowning. He *was* drowning — in his own mediocrity. He grew tired of life.

His friends saw through him. Even strangers did not have time for him, as he was no longer congruent. His purpose had been clear to him since childhood. In the midst of a confusing family life, Gavin had sought knowledge in things that do not readily change, including chemistry, physics and mathematics. He found that his purpose was to make sense of life, and then to help others do the same. He found his purpose as an early childhood teacher.

What matters to Gavin is making sense of life and helping others to do the same. We cannot always find purpose when we have lost it. We can, however, find the part of us that has not forgotten. We may find it through a mystical journey or through a bump on the head.

For some people, it comes through losing someone they loved dearly, perhaps a partner or a child. The loss may come through death or through the end of a relationship. Some awaken to this part of themselves which knows their purpose through deep, searing pain, whereas others do so as a result of a more conscious search. Still others are helped by counsellors, while some find it through prayer or meditation.

It's not lost. You cannot completely lose contact with the part of you that remembers what you have come here to do. If you are observant, you'll notice that your purpose surfaces from time to time in your life, often in periods of change, upheaval or crisis. Once you are consciously aware of your purpose again, there'll be days when you wish you could forget it once more, especially when it calls for sacrifices.

Sometimes it seems that many of us have stopped on the way to fulfilling our purpose. Sasha moved house after 27 years because she felt deep within that she was stagnating. Her move was a recognition that it was time to grow. Four months after moving, she didn't like the new house, and had refused to unpack all of her possessions. She wanted to move back to her old neighbourhood. When she was told (by a clairvoyant) that she wasn't moving back, but instead was moving forward to yet another suburb, she said she didn't want to hear any more about it.

When Sasha was reminded that she had moved initially because of the growing sense of spiritual and emotional emptiness, she nodded in agreement. She recalled the hunger, quiet at first but insistent. 'I've moved, but it hasn't gone away,' she wailed.

'This is the first of several moves, as it is just one more step towards your next long-term home,' she was told. Sasha didn't want to move home again. Many of us are like this. We hope that one step is all it takes to reach our desired goal. Stopping permanently along the way can be as frustrating and unrewarding as remaining where you were when you decided to move.

Maintaining the faith and the courage required to complete the journey is difficult sometimes, but it is necessary. When you discover what you have to share with the world and you begin to offer your gift, we'll all benefit. Whether you directly touch a hundred lives or just one, you'll know in your heart that your gift is worthwhile.

Don't allow anyone to devalue what you give back to the world. It is possible that those who seek to dissuade you from your purpose have difficulty being around someone with purpose. When you have no purpose of your own, it can diminish your self-worth to be close to someone with a strong sense of purpose. Some people who experience this find it easier to dissuade the person close to them from their purpose rather than seek out and pursue their own.

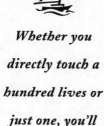

Whether you directly touch a hundred lives or just one, you'll know in your heart that your gift is worthwhile.

Goals are important, but life is more than maintaining a home, a car and a job. Taking from life continually creates a vacuum. We have an innate need to give something back to the community, the country or even the world at large. There is something you can give back, something which only you can give, in your unique way. It's not always easy, but it's almost always worthwhile. The rest of us need what you have to offer.

Your body is your compass; it can guide you to your purpose and to the fulfilment of that purpose. There will still be storms and rough seas, but in the calmer days, your compass is a useful tool on life's journey. This is a compass you cannot lose, yet some of us practise ignoring it or misreading its signals.

You'll complete the journey with or without the aid of your inner compass, but heeding the call of your purpose and following it makes the journey worth all the tempests nature can offer. All life has purpose. Sometimes we need to rediscover that purpose and fulfil it. To begin, you need only to listen, instead, to your quiet inner voice.